Junior Cycle
SPHE

GW00871501

I BELONG
Book 1
26 lessons

Social, Personal and Health Education

Stephanie Mangan

SPHE series in 80 Lessons

An innovative approach to SPHE

FOLENS

Editor

Susan McKeever

Design and layout

Karen Hoey

Cover design

Karen Hoey

Picture research

Susan McKeever

Illustrations

Maria Murray

ISBN: 978-1-84741-979-8

1326

Folens Publishers,

Hibernian Industrial Estate,

Greenhills Road,

Tallaght,

Dublin 24

Acknowledgements

The author and Publisher would like to thank the following for permission to reproduce photographs:

Corbis, Glow Images, Thinkstock, Wikimedia Commons.

Introduction

SPHE stands for **Social, Personal and Health Education**. There are ten modules in this subject, and you will cover these ten modules each year for three years. The ten modules are:

- **Belonging and integrating**
- **Self-management: a sense of purpose**
- **Communication skills**
- **Physical health**
- **Friendship**
- **Relationships and sexuality**
- **Emotional health**
- **Influences and decisions**
- **Substance use**
- **Personal safety**

There are lots of activities in this book that may involve working together or working on your own. There might not always be time to do every activity, so the teacher will decide which activities your class will do. Below are the activity symbols that you will see in the book with an explanation of what each symbol means.

Learning outcome

This symbol shows you things you should know by the end of a particular lesson or module.

Individual work

When you see this symbol, you have to do the work on your own.

Pair work

This means that you work together as a pair. Your teacher will assign you a partner.

Group work

This symbol indicates that this activity should be done in groups. Your teacher will divide you into groups.

Class discussion

This means that the class should discuss a particular topic. Your teacher will lead the discussion.

Homework

This shows the homework for you to complete at home relating to each lesson.

Teacher input

When you see this symbol, teachers have access to additional resources in the Teacher's Resource Book or digital resources on Folensonline. The teacher can access these resources from the eBook on Folensonline for use in the classroom.

Weblink

When you see this symbol, a website will be recommended. You can look this up at home to find out more information on a particular topic.

Contents

Description of modules

In the table below there is a description of each of the ten modules that will be covered this year. Beside each one there is a space for you to fill in the date that you have completed that module. Your parents/guardians might like to read this table to see what you will be learning about in SPHE.

Module	Description	Page	Date of completion
1. Belonging and integrating	Self-esteem depends on lots of things, and feeling secure is one of the most important. This module aims to help you to deal with factors that can affect that security, mainly the move from primary to secondary school.	1	
2. Self management: a sense of purpose	This module focuses on developing good skills for personal organisation and effective work and leisure habits. The importance of teamwork is also covered.	32	
3. Communication skills	The ability to communicate is very important for healthy personal and social development. This module focuses on reinforcing basic skills for self-expression and for listening. You will also be introduced to different types of communication and when they should be used.	45	
4. Physical health	Physical health is just one element of personal health and wellbeing. Other elements – including emotional, sexual and social ones – are covered elsewhere in junior cycle SPHE. This module focuses on lifestyle patterns that are important for good physical health.	57	
5. Friendship	The move to secondary school can separate you from your childhood friends. There is added pressure on students who move from a single-sex into a co-educational environment. This module offers opportunities to explore these issues.	78	

module 1
Belonging and integrating

Self-esteem depends on lots of things, and feeling secure is one of the most important. This module aims to help you to deal with factors that can affect that security, mainly the move from primary to secondary school.

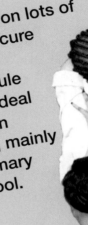

 At the end of this module you will:

- Have thought about your current stage of development.

- Have further developed your group work and communication skills.

- Be more sensitive to your own talents and those of others.

- Be aware of your responsibilities as members of the school community.

- Be aware of the characteristics of bullying behaviour.

- Know the school policy on bullying and be willing to stick to that policy.

- Be able to identify the member of the staff to approach if necessary.

lesson 1
Coping with change 1

At the end of this lesson you will:

★ Recognise the differences between primary and secondary school.

★ Know who to ask for help if you are finding the move from primary to second level difficult.

★ Be aware of the things that worry and excite you and your classmates about your new school.

Opening activity

You have three minutes to find a person in your class who matches the features below. You must write their full name and then get them to sign beside it. You cannot use the same person twice.

Find someone who. . .

Feature	Name	Signature
Plays basketball		
Has brown eyes		
Wears glasses		
Has two or more sisters		
Has no brothers		
Plays football		
Was born in another country		
Has a dog		
Supports Manchester Utd		
Walks to school		
Has blonde hair		
Gets the bus to school		
Is taking French		

Starting secondary school

Starting secondary school is a very exciting time and you probably have lots of hopes or expectations about what it will be like. At the same time, you might be very worried and nervous. The first few weeks can be a bit scary. Last year you were the oldest in your school and the young kids looked up to you. This year you are one of the 'young kids' looking up to the Sixth Years. Some of the biggest fears you might have in the first few weeks of secondary school include:

- ✩ **Bringing the wrong books to class.**
- ✩ **Making new friends.**
- ✩ **Having so many different teachers.**
- ✩ **Starting new subjects.**
- ✩ **Getting into trouble.**
- ✩ **Being hassled by other students.**

In the beginning all of these things might scare you, but by Christmas time you should be settled in and you will have forgotten all of these worries. The following exercises are designed to help you to settle in with your new class and in your new school.

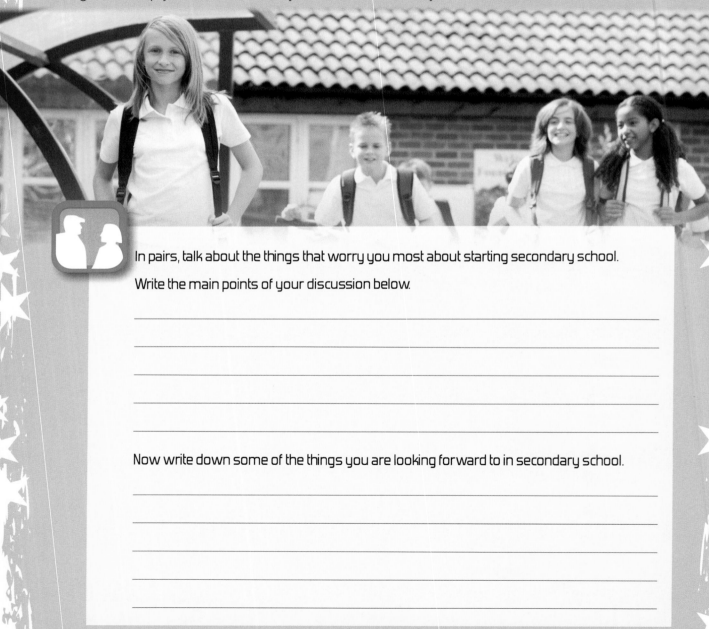

In pairs, talk about the things that worry you most about starting secondary school.

Write the main points of your discussion below.

_____

_____

_____

_____

_____

Now write down some of the things you are looking forward to in secondary school.

_____

_____

_____

_____

_____

_____

Asking for help

With your teacher's help, write down where or who you should go to if:

1. You lose a book, a bag or sports equipment.

2. You are injured or you feel sick.

3. You have a note to leave school early.

4. You were late for school.

5. You have a problem with a subject.

Finding things hard?

If you are finding the move from primary to secondary school very difficult you can always ask somebody for help. You will certainly not be the first person who has found all of these changes overwhelming.

In a group, write a list of people who you could ask for help.

_____

_____

_____

_____

_____

_____

_____

Every day this week you must write something new in the space below that you did in your new school. For example, 'Today I cooked in Home Economics for the first time' or 'Today was the first day that I didn't forget a book'.

Below is a sample *Dear Diary*. You will have to fill in a diary like this after every SPHE lesson to recap on what you learned. You will also be asked to share this *Dear Diary* section with your parents/guardians every week so that they can see what you learned about in SPHE. Showing your parent/guardian your *Dear Diary* can also make it easy for you to ask them questions that you may find difficult to ask normally. Your teacher will let you know if you need to get your *Dear Diary* signed every week.

Sample Dear Diary

Dear Diary...

Date: 9th September 2011

Today's lesson title in SPHE was... coping with change

We learned about... things that are different in our new school. Where to go if we have a problem like losing a book or being late. The things that other people in my class are looking forward to or are worried about.

One interesting topic we discussed was... How some people can actually get sick because they worry so much.

Or... the teacher told us a funny story about when he started secondary school.

Here is something new that I learned... If I have a problem I can make an appointment with the guidance counsellor by just sticking a note under her door. Or I could talk to my mentor in fifth year because she will help me out.

I must remember to talk to my parents/guardians about... How they liked secondary school. I must remember to tell them about the guidance counsellor/mentors/class tutor system.

Parent's/guardian's signature   My signature
J. Kelly   Beth Kelly

lesson 2
Coping with change 2

At the end of this lesson you will:

✿ Understand the changes that some of your classmates may be experiencing.

✿ Know how to deal with change in a positive way.

✿ Have thought about the changes that are happening in your life.

1. Everyone in the class takes turns to introduce themselves or to write their names on the board. Now see if someone can say the names of all the students in the class.

2. Interview the person beside you and find out the most unusual thing you have in common. It might be that you both like cold chips! Present your findings to the class.

Coping with change

This is a time in your life when there are many big changes. Some people find it hard to deal with so many changes all at once and may become stressed or upset. Some of the changes that occur at this time of your life include:

- ☆ **Changes in your body.**
- ☆ **Changes in your feelings and emotions.**
- ☆ **You may be more interested in having a boyfriend or girlfriend.**
- ☆ **Your parents may expect you to take on more responsibility.**
- ☆ **You have to make new friends.**

As all of these things are happening at around the same time, it can be a lot to deal with. Many of the things you will learn about in SPHE – such as communication skills, understanding puberty, friendships, relationships and decision-making – will help you to deal with these changes. The best way to deal with change is to **educate yourself and talk to other people.** Don't forget that your parents and older brothers and sisters went through the same thing when they were your age, so talk to them if you are worried about something. Use the skills and information you learn in SPHE to deal with your feelings. Don't be afraid to ask questions if you don't understand something.

Write a list of big or small changes you have gone through recently.

_____

_____

_____

_____

_____

Seán's story

We will now learn about Seán's story.
In a group, answer these questions.

What problem did Seán have?

_____

_____

How did Seán feel?

_____

_____

List the changes Seán was experiencing.

_____

_____

What advice would you give to Seán?

_____

_____

_____

Pretend that you
are Seán.
Write a positive ending
to his story.

Dear Diary...

Date: _____

Today's lesson title in SPHE was... _____

We learned about... _____

_____

One interesting topic we discussed was... _____

_____

Here is something new that I learned... _____

_____

_____

I must remember to talk to my parents/guardians about... _____

_____

Parent's/guardian's signature _____ My signature _____

_____

Any comments? _____

_____

Comments from teachers or parents/guardians can be written here but this does not have to be filled in every week.

lesson 3
Joining a new group

At the end of this lesson you will:

Know more about your new school so that you can be a responsible member of the school community.

Know something new about your classmates.

Opening activity

Say your name and one interesting thing about yourself. The next person repeats what you said and adds their own name and something about themselves. Continue this until everyone in the class has introduced themselves. For example: 'John likes basketball, Sonia is from Lithuania, my name is Joe and I support Arsenal.'

There is a seating plan for your class below. Fill in the full names of your classmates on this plan. If you have an unusual or difficult name, write it on the board (with the teacher's permission). You may need to teach your classmates and teacher how to pronounce it properly too.

Teacher's desk

Knowing your classmates

By now you should have met most of the people in your class and should know at least one thing about each of them. It is important that you try to get to know the people in your class properly because you will be spending a lot of time with them. To make new friends you should:

- ✿ **Be friendly, smile and say hello.**
- ✿ **Be helpful. Show them where their class is or lend them a pen or similar if they need it.**
- ✿ **Talk to them at break time.**
- ✿ **Join sports teams or take part in school activities such as plays.**
- ✿ **Ask a person questions about themselves to show you are interested.**
- ✿ **Try to remember people's names – do this by saying the name when you speak to them.**
- ✿ **If you are bad at remembering names, write them down somewhere.**
- ✿ **Don't ignore someone just because they have a disability or are a different race to you. They could end up being one of your best friends.**

Getting to know your new school

It is important that you find out as much as you can about your new school so that you can become a part of the school community. One of the biggest changes in secondary school is having new subjects and lots of different teachers.

Fill in the table below with a list of your subjects and your teachers' names. Tick the 'new' column if you have never done this subject before. Tick the 'old' column if you have done it before.

Subject	Teacher	New	Old

School rules

School rules are important – they stop the school from being chaotic. If there were no rules, everyone could do what they liked and get away with it. School rules are in place to ensure that students are disciplined fairly, and so they know what to expect when they do something wrong. You will probably have a copy of the school rules in your journal. Everyone should take the time to read all of these rules. Ask your teacher if you are unsure about what a particular rule means. It is your responsibility to follow these rules at all times so that everyone gets an opportunity to learn. This is their right.

Working in pairs, write out the rules in your new school that are different from the ones you had in primary school. Use the space below.

_____
_____
_____
_____
_____
_____
_____

Fill in the details of your school below. There is a space for you to draw in your school emblem. Some of the information may be in your school journal, or a teacher may help you with the things you don't know.

School emblem

School name: _____

Address: _____

Telephone number: _____

Number of students: _____

Number of First Years: _____

Number of teachers: _____

Age of school: _____

Name of principal: _____

Name of vice-principal: _____

Type of school: _____

Dear Diary...

Date: _____

Today's lesson title in SPHE was... _____

_____

We learned about... _____

_____

_____

One interesting topic we discussed was... _____

_____

_____

Here is something new that I learned... _____

_____

_____

I must remember to talk to my parents/guardians about... _____

_____

_____

_____

_____   _____

Parent's/guardian's signature   My signature

_____

Any comments? _____

_____

_____

Comments from teachers or parents/guardians can be written here but this <u>does not</u> have to be filled in every week.

lesson 4
Appreciating difference

At the end of this lesson you will:

★ Recognise your own gifts and talents and the gifts and talents of others.

★ Have learned how to work well in a group.

Form groups of five or six. One person in the group must think of a famous person but not tell anyone who it is. The others in the group must take turns to ask questions to find out who it is, but the answer can only be yes or no. If someone thinks they know, they can have a guess but if they are wrong they are out. Once 20 questions have been asked, then everyone loses. If someone guesses correctly, they win.

Difference is good

Everybody in your class is unique and each person has their own special gifts or talents. Some people may be good at sport or skilled at music; some may have a good sense of humour or be good listeners. Other people are great at making people feel special or have a great imagination. It is these different gifts and talents that make each of us unique.

List two gifts or talents that you have.

_____

_____

_____

_____

Find out one gift or talent the person beside you has.

_____

_____

Working in a group

During SPHE and many other subjects, you will often be put into groups for an activity or project. Group work relies on the gifts and talents of each individual. Some may be good at organising or listening; others may be good at problem solving or note taking.

It is important to establish some ground rules for group work. The main thing is that everyone in the group has a chance to talk. The group or your teacher can choose someone to present the group's findings to the class. Sometimes the group or your teacher might choose a **chairperson**.

The chairperson's job is to:

1. Remind the group of how much time is left for the discussion.
2. Make sure everyone has a chance to speak.
3. Ask if everyone agrees before you all write something down.

As a class, discuss and then set the ground rules for group work in SPHE. Then fill in the contract on the next page.

Suggested rules

✩ Not to laugh at other people's opinions.

✩ To take part in group work.

✩ To use 'I' statements (such as 'I feel' and 'I think', so that people know it is only my personal opinion).

Suggested discipline for breaking a rule

✩ Take a five-minute 'Time Out' if I am being rude or disruptive.

✩ Lose the chance to take part in group work if I am messing.

✩ Apologise if I hurt someone's feelings.

CONTRACT FOR SPHE CLASS

I promise...

_____
_____
_____
_____
_____
_____
_____
_____
_____

If I break a rule, I will...

_____
_____
_____
_____
_____
_____
_____
_____
_____
_____
_____

Signed _____

Date _____

Now you can put your group work skills to the test. Read the following story and as a group answer the question.

As the jealous, controlling king left, he warned his wife: 'Do not leave the castle while I am gone, or I will punish you severely when I return!'

But as the hours passed, the young queen grew lonely, and despite her husband's warning, decided to visit her friend, who lived in the countryside nearby.

The castle was located on an island in a wide, fast-flowing river, with a drawbridge linking the island and the land at the narrowest point in the river.

'Surely my husband will not return before dawn,' she thought, and she ordered her servants to lower the drawbridge and leave it down until she returned.

After spending the afternoon with her friend, the queen returned to the drawbridge, only to find it blocked by the king's most faithful servant wildly waving a stick at her. 'Do not attempt to cross this bridge,' he raved. 'I know that you have disobeyed the king's orders.'

Fearing for her life, the queen escaped his grip and ran back to her friend to ask him to help.

'I cannot risk going near the castle. If anyone finds out about you coming here, the king will kill me, and I do not want to take that risk,' he said. 'I will not help.'

The queen then sought out a boatman on the river, explained her problem to him, and asked him to take her across the river in his boat.

'I will do it, but only if you can pay my fee of five gold coins.'

'But I have no money with me!' the queen protested.

'That is too bad. I will not take you then,' the boatman said flatly.

Her fears growing, the queen ran crying to her mother's house, and after again explaining the situation, she begged for enough money to pay the boatman his fee. Her mother also feared the controlling, angry king.

'If you had not disobeyed your husband, this would not have happened,' her mother said. 'I will give you no money.'

With dawn approaching, and her last resource exhausted, the queen returned to the bridge in desperation. As she attempted to cross to the castle the king's loyal servant sneaked up behind her, waving his stick. The queen lost her footing as she tried to escape him and fell to her death in the deep river below. When the king returned and heard the terrible news, he vowed to hunt down and punish anybody who was responsible for the death of his wife.

In the story there are six characters:

1. The queen   **2.** The mother   **3.** The king

4. The friend   **5.** The boatman   **6.** The king's loyal servant

Now your group must rank each character according to how responsible he or she was for the queen's death. Rank the characters from 1 to 6, with 1 being the most responsible and 6 being the least responsible. Make sure to follow the ground rules for group work and elect a chairperson. Discuss your findings with the class.

What gift or talent did you use in the group work today?

_____

What other gifts or talents did you notice other people in your group using?

_____

_____

This week, observe people you know and find out one talent that they have. Don't ask them — just figure it out yourself. When you discover a talent they have, you can tell them and then write it in the table below. For example: 'Mum, did you know that you are a very good listener ?'

Person				
Talent				

Dear Diary...

Date: _____

Today's lesson title in SPHE was... _____

We learned about... _____

_____

One interesting topic we discussed was... _____

_____

Here is something new that I learned... _____

_____

I must remember to talk to my parents/guardians about... _____

_____

_____

Parent's/guardian's signature _____   My signature _____

Any comments? _____

_____

Comments from teachers or parents/guardians can be written here but this <u>does not</u> have to be filled in every week.

lesson 5
Bullying is everyone's business 1

At the end of this lesson you will:

Understand what bullying is.

Identify different types of bullying behaviour.

Your teacher will put up an **Agree** and a **Disagree** sign in different corners of the classroom. Stand at the right place in the classroom according to whether you agree or disagree with, the following statements.

- ✪ Bullying is more common in secondary schools than in primary schools.
- ✪ Bullying is more common among girls.
- ✪ A bully is a strong, tough person.
- ✪ A bully's victim is usually small and weak.
- ✪ Bullying is becoming more common than it used to be.
- ✪ Being bullied is a good way to toughen up a person.

Bullying

Bullying is aggressive behaviour by a person or a group of people against others. It is usually deliberate and repeated.

Discuss as a class what is meant by this definition.

A group of First Year boys discuss bullying. Answer the questions that follow.

1. What types of bullying are mentioned?

2. Do you agree with Patricia Kennedy that reality TV shows encourage young people to make nasty or hurtful remarks?

3. Do you agree that there is a huge pressure on teenagers to 'conform' or act in a particular way?

Types of bullying

☆ **Physical bullying:** Hitting, pushing, tripping, spitting, stealing, vandalising or damaging property.

☆ **Verbal bullying:** Name-calling, taunting, slagging, threatening, daring others to do things they know are dangerous or wrong.

☆ **Psychological bullying:** Excluding, ridiculing, spreading rumours, passing notes, using peer pressure to intimidate, setting others up for humiliation, using threatening gestures or looks.

☆ **Sexual bullying:** Unwelcome sexual comments, unwelcome touching, spreading rumours about a person's sexual orientation.

☆ **Racist bullying:** Discrimination, prejudice, comments about colour, nationality, ethnicity or Traveller background.

☆ **Relational bullying:** Manipulating relationships, for example ignoring, excluding from the peer group, talking loudly enough so that the victim can hear their name being mentioned, demeaning looks, abusive notes or drawings. Cyber bullying is a form of relational bullying, and includes abusive phone calls, text messages, emails and posts on social networking sites.

Is this bullying?

For each of the situations below, answer the question: *'Is this bullying?'* Tick yes, no or not sure. If you answer yes, say what type of bullying it is.

		Yes	No	Not sure
1.	Every time Sabita answers a question in class she can hear the students behind her whispering, copying her accent and giggling.			
Type:				
2.	John fell off his chair in the lunch room and everyone around him laughed.			
Type:				
3.	Carly keeps finding hurtful stuff written about her on the doors in the school toilets.			
Type:				
4.	Peter is always getting spiteful messages on his Facebook page about being gay.			
Type:				
5.	Laura tripped over her classmate's bag in the corridor and broke her wrist when she fell.			
Type:				
6.	Nobody sits beside Ciarán in class and he eats his lunch by himself.			
Type:				

		Yes	No	Not sure
7.	Mark and Liam never ask Ian to go to the pictures with them anymore.			
Type:				
8.	Áine's books keep going missing and someone poured paint from the art room on her schoolbag.			
Type:				
9.	When Lisa is changing for PE, Ciara and Claire make coughing noises and hold their noses.			
Type:				
10.	Tom whispers to Daniel that he is 'going to get him' every time he passes him in the corridor.			
Type:				
11.	Aisling told everyone a secret that Ellen told her last year about her mother being an alcoholic.			
Type:				
12.	Mr Byrne gives out to Shane every day because he doesn't do his homework and is always putting him on detention for this.			
Type:				

Bullying quiz

Answer true or false to the following statements. In some cases, you might have to guess the answer. Once everyone has completed the quiz, your teacher will tell you the correct answers.

		True	False
1.	Only one in five students who are bullied tells their teachers about it.		
2.	Spreading rumours about someone is a type of bullying.		
3.	Three-quarters of children who are being bullied tell their parents.		
4.	Ignoring someone is a type of bullying.		
5.	16 per cent of secondary school students have been bullied at one time.		
6.	A teacher can bully a student.		
7.	The most common place for secondary school students to be bullied is in the corridors.		
8.	A student can bully a teacher.		

Give an example of the following types of bullying. The first one has been done for you.

Racist bullying: _Christine slags Eileen about living in a caravan._

Psychological bullying: _____

_____

Verbal bullying: _____

_____

Sexual bullying: _____

_____

Physical bullying: _____

_____

Relational bullying: _____

Define bullying in your own words.

_____

_____

For class next week, read your school's anti-bullying policy. This may be in your homework diary or on your school website.

Dear Diary...

Date: _____

Today's lesson title in SPHE was... _____

_____

We learned about... _____

_____

_____

One interesting topic we discussed was... _____

_____

Here is something new that I learned... _____

_____

_____

I must remember to talk to my parents/guardians about... _____

Parent's/guardian's signature _____   My signature _____

Any comments? _____

_____

Comments from teachers or parents/guardians can be written here but this does not have to be filled in every week.

lesson 6
Bullying is everyone's business 2

At the end of this lesson you will:

Be aware of your school's policy on bullying.

Know how to tell someone if you or someone else is being bullied.

The teacher will whisper a message into a student's ear. The student passes the message on by whispering to the person on their left. They can only whisper the message once. The last person to hear the message must say the message aloud.

How to tell

If you or someone you know is being bullied you must tell an adult as they can help you deal with it properly. You will not be in trouble for telling the truth. Your school will have an anti-bullying policy – you can probably find it in your homework journal or on the school website. Read this policy with your teacher then answer these questions.

Who should you tell about bullying?

_____

_____

What happens to me if I am being bullied?

_____

_____

What happens to the bully?

_____

_____

In pairs, come up with a list of other ways you can tell if you are being bullied.

_____

_____

_____

_____

_____

_____

Part 1:

The image below is taken from the ISPCC Anti-Bullying Awareness Campaign. Examine the poster, which shows Mark Feehily of Westlife fame, and then answer the questions which follow.

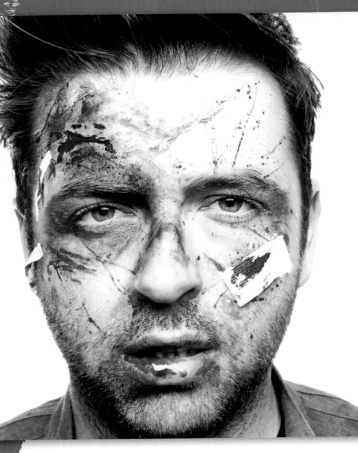

ISPCC
ALWAYS HERE FOR CHILDREN

" **Imagine if every child went to sleep without fearing what the next day would bring.** "

JOIN THE FIGHT FOR CHILDREN'S RIGHTS.
ISPCC.IE

1. How does this poster make you feel?

_____

_____

_____

2. What is the main message of this poster?

_____

_____

_____

To find out more about this campaign and to see pictures of other people who took part, such as Jedward and Louis Walsh, go to **www.ispcc.ie**.

Part 2:

In the space below write a letter to your school principal. The teacher may choose the best letter from the class to give to the principal. Report to him or her on the following:

☆ Do you think there is much bullying in this school?

☆ What type of bullying happens most often in this school?

☆ What does your group think about the school's policy on bullying?

☆ Do you have any suggestions on how the school's policy on bullying can be improved?

☆ Does your group have any suggestions that may help stop bullying?

Design a leaflet for first years to inform them about bullying and to tell them what to do if they or someone they know is being bullied. Go to **www.ispcc.ie** and find the 2011 Anti-Bullying Awareness Campaign to help you with this.

Dear Diary...

Date: _____

Today's lesson title in SPHE was... _____
_____

We learned about... _____
_____
_____

One interesting topic we discussed was... _____
_____
_____

Here is something new that I learned... _____
_____
_____

I must remember to talk to my parents/guardians about... _____
_____
_____
_____

_____   _____
Parent's/guardian's signature   My signature

Any comments? _____
_____
_____

Comments from teachers or parents/guardians can be written here but this does not have to be filled in every week.

module 2
Self-management: a sense of purpose

This module focuses on developing good skills for personal organisation and effective work and leisure habits. The importance of teamwork is also covered.

At the end of this module you will:

Be able to plan and organise your school and homework efficiently.

Have a greater awareness of the importance of teamwork.

Have a broadened vision of what it means to be healthy.

lesson 7
Organising myself at home and at school

At the end of this lesson you will:

☆ Understand the importance of planning and preparation.

☆ Be able to plan and organise your school and homework more efficiently.

In groups of five, organise yourselves in a line according to your age, without talking.

Organising yourself

Some people may find the planning and organisation that is needed in secondary school quite difficult. You need to plan ahead or prepare for many things such as PE, home economics, school trips, homework and tests.

Below are some tips to help you be prepared. Read them, and then in groups add more tips to the list.

1. Always write your homework in your diary at the end of each class.

2. If doing cooking in home economics, tell your parent/guardian the ingredients you need the week before, not the night before (when the shops may be closed).

_____

_____

_____

_____

Keeping your room reasonably tidy will ensure you don't lose stuff you need.

Pamela's story

We will now learn about Pamela's story.
In pairs, answer the questions that follow.

1. Why did Pamela change her approach to study?

2. Describe two changes Pamela made to her usual routine to incorporate study.

3. Describe two methods Pamela used to study.

4. Suggest two other methods that Pamela could use to help her study.

Note taking

One method of studying is note taking. If you start taking or making notes now, you can use them to study and revise for your summer tests and for your Junior Certificate. Try to make some notes every day on what you did in each subject. The purpose of notes is to sum up what you have learned so that you won't have to read the whole textbook again when you get to Third Year. Follow the guidelines below for taking notes.

Write a heading

- Use bullet points.
- Use short sentences.
- Underline the important points.
- Highlight the important words.
- Use symbols instead of long words.
- Write the lesson/chapter and page number at the end for reference. (Lesson 7, page 36)

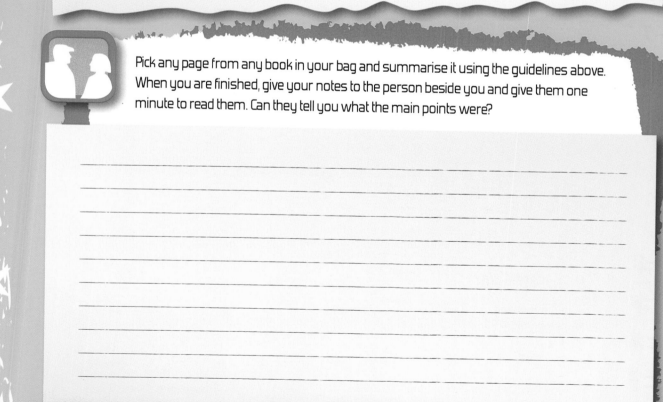

Pick any page from any book in your bag and summarise it using the guidelines above. When you are finished, give your notes to the person beside you and give them one minute to read them. Can they tell you what the main points were?

Try out new methods of studying this week, such as the ones you suggested for Pamela. In the space below, write about the method that works well for you.

_____

_____

_____

_____

_____

_____

_____

_____

_____

Dear Diary...

Date: _____

Today's lesson title in SPHE was...

_____

We learned about...

_____

_____

One interesting topic we discussed was...

_____

_____

Here is something new that I learned...

_____

_____

I must remember to talk to my parents/guardians about...

_____

_____

Parent's/guardian's signature   My signature

_____

Any comments?

_____

_____

Comments from teachers or parents/guardians can be written here but this <u>does not</u> have to be filled in every week.

A balanced lifestyle

Along with eating well and exercising, relaxation is vital for a balanced lifestyle. Everyone relaxes in different ways, so it is important to find a method of relaxation that works for you. Your relaxation or leisure time could be active such as walking, fishing or dancing. On the other hand, it could be inactive such as reading, using the internet or watching TV. If you don't take the time to relax, it can lead to stress. Too much stress is unhealthy and can lead to physical and mental illness.

Which do you think is most beneficial to teenagers – active or inactive leisure? Why?

Time chart

Look at the bar chart below, which shows how one teenager spent the day. Use the bar charts on the following page to show how much time you spend on active/inactive leisure, sleeping, eating, doing homework, training or anything else you might do. It doesn't have to add up to a full 24 hours because you are not including things like washing, dressing and travelling. One chart is for the weekend and one is for a school day. Don't forget to add a key, which explains what each colour stands for!

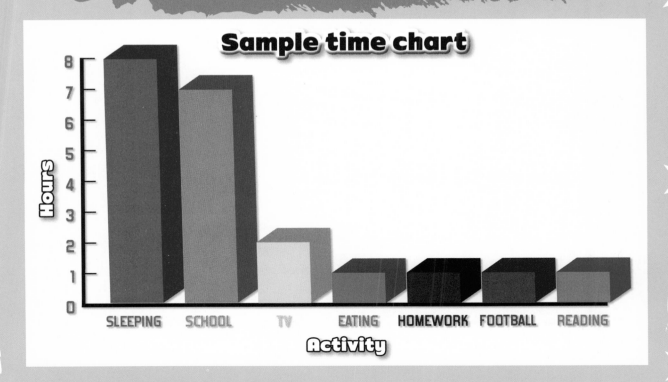

Sample time chart

Weekday time chart

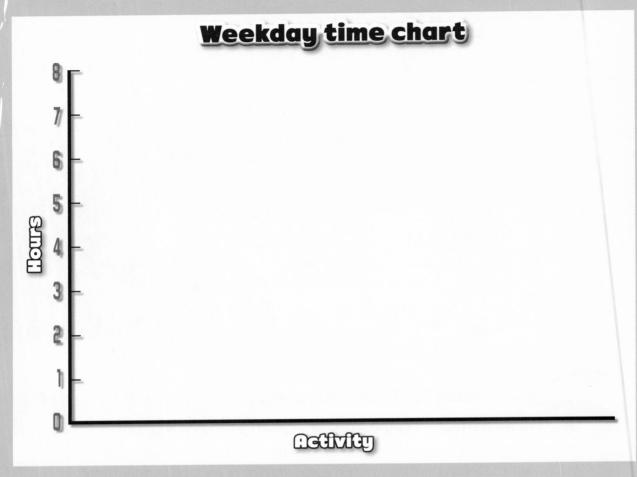

Hours

8
7
6
5
4
3
2
1
0

Activity

Weekend time chart

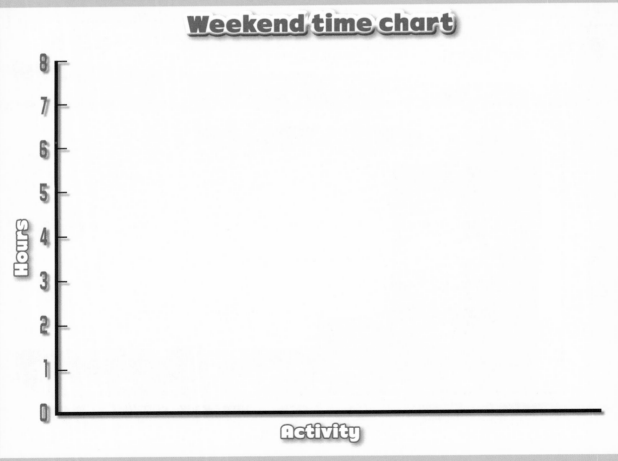

Hours

8
7
6
5
4
3
2
1
0

Activity

Class survey

What is the average amount of time spent the class spends on the following?

- ☆ Active leisure
- ☆ Inactive leisure
- ☆ Sleeping
- ☆ Homework or study

Look at the results for the class survey. Are you above or below average for each activity?

What changes could you make to improve how you spend your time?

_____

_____

_____

_____

_____

_____

Interview your partner to find out how she or he likes to relax. Ask the following questions.

1. What is your favourite way to relax?

2. Why do you like this activity?

3. Do you have any other hobbies or interests that help you to relax?

Teens like 'addicts' without gadgets

By Nick Bramhill, The Irish Examiner, Thursday, January 6, 2011

1. TEENS are becoming so addicted to texting and surfing the net that they behave like recovering drug addicts when forced to switch their gadgets off, research has found. Researchers have discovered that the 'Net Generation' of teenagers and young adults are so hooked on their mobiles and computers that they display withdrawal symptoms similar to those seen in drug users trying to go 'cold turkey'.

2. A leading Irish parents' organisation last night said the findings prove how over-reliant many youngsters have become on modern technology. For the study, an international team of researchers asked volunteers to stay away from all emails, text messages, Facebook and Twitter updates for 24 hours. They found that the participants began to develop symptoms typically seen in smokers attempting to give up.

3. Some of the subjects taking part said they felt like they were undergoing 'cold turkey' to break a hard drug habit, while others said it felt like going on a diet. The condition is being described as Information Deprivation Disorder.
   In the experiment, called Unplugged, volunteers at 12 universities around the world spent 24 hours without access to computers, mobiles, iPods, TV, radio and even newspapers. However, they were allowed to use landline phones or read books.

4. The study, led by the University of Maryland's International Centre for Media and the Public Agenda, encouraged participants to keep diaries about their experiences. Entries in the diaries showed that many recorded feeling fidgety, anxious or isolated. Last night the National Parents' Council (post-primary) director Catherine Riordan said she was sure the average teenager would struggle if forced to live without their technology. And she said that she recognised the symptoms displayed by participants in real-life situations when parents had tried to limit the time their kids spent online. However, Ms Riordan said online addiction is not limited to teenagers. She said: 'Whole families can be at home together, each in separate rooms on separate devices and barely interact with each other. I know of mothers who find that the best way to get a response from their kids is to send a text or Facebook message.'

Discuss the newspaper article and pick out words that you would associate with 'addiction'. Could you go on a 24-hour technology fast? Perhaps the whole class could? Report back next week on how you felt and what you did.

In pairs, come up with a heading for each paragraph in the above article.

Keep a time log of how you spend your time this week.

	Active leisure	Inactive leisure	Sleeping	Homework/ study
Monday				
Tuesday				
Wednesday				
Thursday				
Friday				
Saturday				
Sunday				

Dear Diary...

Date: _____

Today's lesson title in SPHE was... _____

We learned about... _____
_____

One interesting topic we discussed was... _____
_____

Here is something new that I learned... _____
_____

I must remember to talk to my parents/guardians about... _____
_____
_____

Parent's/guardian's signature _____   My signature _____

Any comments? _____
_____

Comments from teachers or parents/guardians can be written here but this <u>does not</u> have to be filled in every week.

module 3
Communication skills

The ability to communicate is very important for healthy personal and social development. This module focuses on reinforcing basic skills for self-expression and for listening. You will also be introduced to different types of communication and when they should be used.

At the end of this module you will:

Have learned and practised the skills of listening and of self-expression.

Be more aware of the need to be sensitive to the opinions of others.

Know and understand different types of communication.

Be aware of the appropriateness of different types of communication.

Have learned skills to solve conflicts.

lesson 9
Expressing myself and learning to listen

At the end of this lesson you will:

★ Have developed your listening skills.

★ Be more aware of the need to be sensitive to the opinions of others.

★ Understand how you express yourself verbally and non-verbally.

Three people are blindfolded at one side of the classroom. Using communication, three others guide the blindfolded people to them at the other side of the classroom. The other students pick out the best listener and the best communicator and explain why.

Respecting the opinions of others

You may not always agree with other peoples' opinions but you should still be sensitive to their views. You can show respect by listening to them and asking questions about things that you don't understand or that you disagree with. Use phrases such as 'I feel', 'I think' or 'in my opinion'. The activity you just did highlights the importance of listening. You must be a good listener to be a good communicator. If someone is sharing their opinion with you, they can tell if you are not listening. This is rude and disrespectful, so they will probably stop sharing their thoughts and opinions with you in the future.

Discuss the following as a class:

1. How can you tell that someone is not listening to you?

2. How does it make you feel when someone does not listen to you (for example, a parent, a teacher or a friend)?

List some characteristics of a good listener.

_____

_____

_____

_____

_____

Expressing yourself

When you were younger you could just cry to let someone know when you were hurt, or scream if you got frustrated. As you get older you learn other ways to express how you feel. You can express your feelings **verbally** or **non-verbally**.

Expressing feelings **verbally** means you say what it is you want to express.

Expressing feelings **non-verbally** means you use body language or facial expressions – for example, frowning, slouching and glaring – to express yourself.

In pairs, discuss what the following gestures usually mean and then write in your answers.

1. Folding your arms when someone is talking to you.

_____

2. Avoiding eye contact when talking to someone.

_____

3. Smiling and looking into someone's eyes when you talk to them.

_____

4. Raising your eyebrows when listening to someone.

_____

5. Yawning when someone is speaking to you.

_____

6. Looking around you or at your watch when someone is speaking to you.

_____

7. Biting your fingernails when someone is speaking to you.

_____

8. Looking at someone and nodding when they are speaking to you.

_____

9. Slouching in your chair when someone is speaking to you.

_____

10. Touching someone on the arm as you speak to him or her.

_____

Do you know your own body language? Try to answer the following questions. If other pupils in the class know you well, they might be able to help you.

What do you do when you are...?

Nervous: _____

Worried: _____

Excited: _____

Bored: _____

Communication skills

Here are some general tips on how to share your feelings with other people.

✿ **Be assertive.** This means saying clearly what you want or what you feel, without shouting or hurting the other person's feelings.

✿ **Don't be aggressive.** If you shout at someone or make sarcastic or rude remarks, you will come across as being aggressive. This isn't good, firstly because you won't get your feelings across clearly and secondly because people won't like you very much for it.

✿ **Don't be passive.** This means even though you know what you want or want to say, you don't actually do anything about it. Sometimes you can be passive by dropping subtle hints in the hope that you will be understood, instead of just saying what you mean.

✿ **Make eye contact.** Look the person you are trying to talk to in the eye. This is very important because it shows them that you are sincere. If looking someone in the eye makes you nervous, try practising in the mirror or practise it when talking to a younger brother or sister.

✿ **Listen.** To be a good communicator you have to be a good listener. Give the other person a chance to respond to what you said. Remember, the other person's feelings or opinions are just as important as yours.

✿ **Write it down.** If you have something very difficult to say to someone and you can't bring yourself to do it, you could try writing it down first. If it's something important, don't write it in a text message or say it over the phone because that's just being cowardly.

✿ **Use assertive body language.**

Look at the following pictures. In groups of four, discuss what the person's body language tells you about him or her.

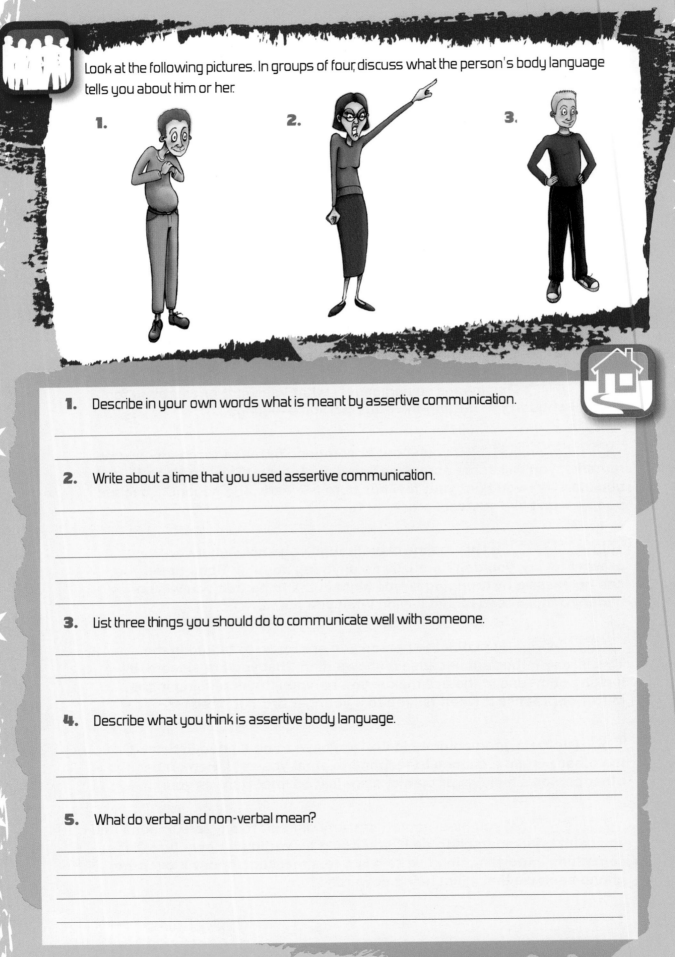

1.

2.

3.

1. Describe in your own words what is meant by assertive communication.
_____
_____

2. Write about a time that you used assertive communication.
_____
_____
_____
_____
_____
_____

3. List three things you should do to communicate well with someone.
_____
_____
_____

4. Describe what you think is assertive body language.
_____
_____
_____

5. What do verbal and non-verbal mean?
_____
_____
_____
_____

Resolving conflict

Conflict or disagreements are part of everyday life. There will often be times where you are upset or annoyed by things that someone has said or done, or when someone disagrees with you. These things can lead to conflict. Think of times in your life when there is conflict. It is important to use your communication skills to help resolve conflict. The best way to do this is by listening and being assertive.

In pairs, complete the following exercise on dealing with conflict.

You arrange to meet your friends at nine o'clock at Lisa's house to go to the disco. You arrive at nine and nobody is home. You wait half an hour and nobody turns up, so you walk to the disco by yourself. When you get there all your friends are there having a good time dancing – they wave and say hello. You wonder if you got the time wrong or if they did this to you on purpose.

How would the following people react?

(A) A passive person

_____

_____

_____

_____

(B) An assertive person

_____

_____

_____

_____

(C) An aggressive person

_____

_____

_____

_____

Write two ways in which you can become a more assertive communicator,
for example 'If I strongly disagree with something, I will say so'.

_____

_____

_____

_____

Dear Diary...

Date: _____

Today's lesson title in SPHE was... _____

_____

We learned about... _____

_____

_____

One interesting topic we discussed was... _____

_____

_____

Here is something new that I learned... _____

_____

_____

I must remember to talk to my parents/guardians about... _____

_____

_____

_____

Parent's/guardian's signature   My signature

_____

Any comments? _____

_____

_____

Comments from teachers or parents/guardians can be written here but this <u>does not</u> have to be filled in every week.

module 4
Physical health

Physical health is just one element of personal health and wellbeing. Other elements – including emotional, sexual and social ones – are covered elsewhere in junior cycle SPHE. This module focuses on lifestyle patterns that are important for good physical health.

At the end of this module you will:

- Know how important personal hygiene is for self-esteem and confidence.

- Understand what is meant by a balanced diet and the effect it has on general health and wellbeing.

- Know the importance of physical exercise, rest and sleep.

- Have made a personal plan for exercise in your own lives.

lesson 11
Body care

At the end of this lesson you will:

Understand the importance of personal hygiene.

Understand skin problems associated with puberty.

Develop skills for maintaining healthy skin, teeth and hair.

On the 'Word Wall' below, write anything that comes to mind when you think about body care. Use colours and symbols or pictures as well as words. Be as creative as you can.

BODY CARE

Personal hygiene

When you become a teenager your sweat glands start to produce more sweat. Perspiration (or sweating) is a natural response from your body to try to cool you down. If you are exercising or nervous your body gets hot, so, in response, your body releases tiny droplets of water. These cool the surface of the skin. Sweat does not smell on its own but when it mixes with the bacteria on your body or if it is not washed away, it will smell and cause body odour.

How to avoid body odour (BO)

- Wash with hot water and soap every day. Pay special attention to your armpits, as sweat will cling to any hair in this area.

- Use a soap that is not perfumed because the perfume destroys some of the good bacteria on your skin.

- Change all of your underwear every day.

- Have a shower or bath at least three times a week and wash every other day.

- Wear cotton underwear and socks because cotton lets your skin breathe. Synthetic fabrics, such as polyester, will trap sweat and make it stay on your skin.

- Put on anti-perspirant, not just deodorant, after you have washed. An anti-perspirant stops you from sweating as much and a deodorant stops the sweat from smelling. Check the bottle to make sure it contains both.

Discuss as a class how your skin and your skin care routine have changed during puberty compared to when you were a child.

Take a few minutes to study the diagram of the skin. Now draw and label your own diagram of the skin.

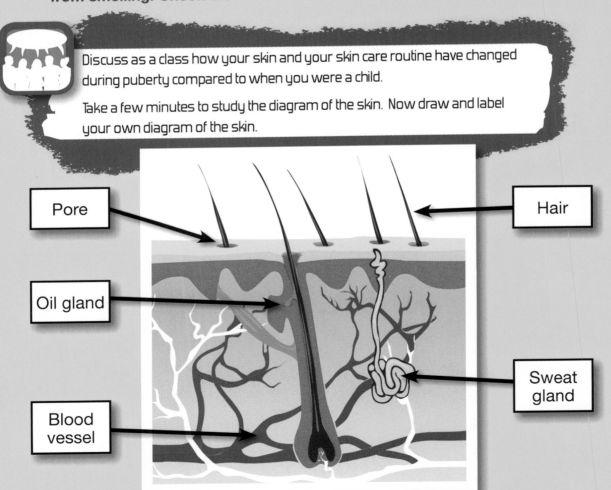

Pore

Hair

Oil gland

Sweat gland

Blood vessel

Dietary recall analysis

Now you must analyse what you ate. If you had a brown bread sandwich with butter and ham, that is one portion from the cereal, bread and potato group, one portion from the meat group and one portion from the others group in the food pyramid.

Group	Number of portions I had	Recommended portions
Others		
Meat, fish and alternatives		
Milk and dairy		
Fruit and vegetables		
Bread, cereals and potatoes		

After analysing your diet, you will see what foods you are not eating enough of and what foods you eat too much of.

Write below how you can make some changes to improve your diet. For example, 'I will have a glass of orange juice with my breakfast'. Don't write things down that you are not going to do – be realistic and keep the changes simple.

1. _____

2. _____

3. _____

4. _____

5. _____

Dear Diary...

Date: _____

Today's lesson title in SPHE was... _____

_____

We learned about... _____

_____

_____

One interesting topic we discussed was... _____

_____

_____

Here is something new that I learned... _____

_____

_____

I must remember to talk to my parents/guardians about... _____

_____

_____

_____

Parent's/guardian's signature _____   My signature _____

_____

Any comments? _____

_____

_____

Comments from teachers or parents/guardians can be written here but this does not have to be filled in every week.

Dear Diary...

Date: _____

Today's lesson title in SPHE was... _____

We learned about... _____
_____
_____

One interesting topic we discussed was... _____
_____
_____

Here is something new that I learned... _____
_____
_____

I must remember to talk to my parents/guardians about... _____
_____
_____

Parent's/guardian's signature _____   My signature _____

Any comments? _____
_____
_____

Comments from teachers or parents/guardians can be written here but this does not have to be filled in every week.

module 5

Friendship

The move to secondary school can separate you from your childhood friends. There is added pressure on students who move from a single-sex into a co-educational environment. This module offers opportunities to explore these issues.

At the end of this module you will:

- Be aware of the nature of friendship.

- Have examined what the qualities of a good friend are.

Write a positive ending to
Clare's story.

Dear Diary...

Date: _____

Today's lesson title in SPHE was... _____

_____

We learned about... _____

_____

_____

One interesting topic we discussed was... _____

_____

_____

Here is something new that I learned... _____

_____

_____

I must remember to talk to my parents/guardians about... _____

_____

_____

_____

Parent's/guardian's signature   My signature

Any comments? _____

_____

_____

Comments from teachers or parents/guardians can be written here but this does not have to be filled in every week.

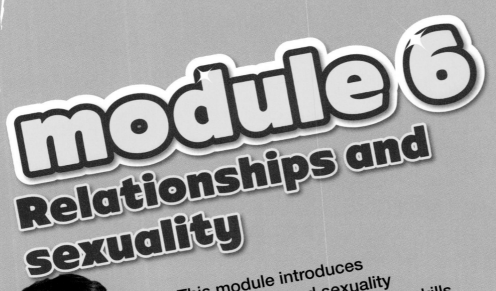

module 6
Relationships and sexuality

This module introduces relationships and sexuality education and gives you the skills needed to cope with changes experienced during adolescence.

At the end of this module you will:

- Appreciate your personal talents and those of others.

- Have explored sex stereotyping.

- Know about the physical, emotional and psychological changes that happen during adolescence.

- Understand the male and female reproductive systems.

- Be aware of the need for respect for one's own sexuality and the sexuality of others.

lesson 15
Me as unique and different

At the end of this lesson you will:

Have reflected on what makes you different.

Have reflected on respect and self-esteem.

Have developed skills for improving your self-esteem.

Each person in the classroom should fill out the profile below. The teacher will read out some of the profiles and others in the class must guess whose profile it is.

facebook Search Home Profile Find friends Account

Age: _____

Hair colour: _____

Eye colour: _____

Favourite food: _____

Favourite movie: _____

Favourite subject: _____

Least favourite subject: _____

Hobbies: _____

The best day I ever had was: _____

Pet hates: _____

Ambition: _____

Self-esteem

In order to respect yourself, you must develop a healthy self-esteem. Your self-esteem is how you value yourself. People with a very negative view of themselves have a poor or unhealthy self-esteem. They find it very hard to deal with any type of criticism and may 'act' in front of other people because they don't feel comfortable being themselves.

People with a positive self-esteem are able to deal with criticism and are comfortable being themselves. You can develop a healthy self-esteem by looking closely at your own personality and knowing what your strengths and weaknesses are. Nobody is perfect and no matter what you do, you never will be perfect. You have to learn to love yourself despite your weaknesses. Loving or respecting yourself doesn't mean you walk around thinking you are better than everyone else. It just means that you like being you and you don't spend your time wishing you were someone else.

As a class, come up with a list of strengths and weaknesses in people's personalities and write them below.

Strengths	Weaknesses

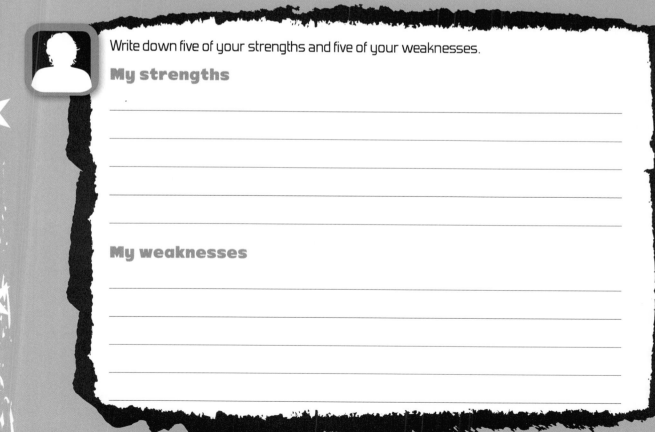

Write down five of your strengths and five of your weaknesses.

My strengths

_____
_____
_____
_____
_____

My weaknesses

_____
_____
_____
_____
_____

What I like about me

Complete these sentences about yourself. Don't be afraid to praise yourself – it doesn't make you big headed, it's just an exercise to help you realise what a great person you are!

1. My best skill or talent is _____

2. I'm not really good at _____ but I enjoy it.

3. I sometimes help my parents by _____

4. I am a good friend because I _____

5. I am really proud of _____

6. The nicest thing I ever did for someone was _____

7. I am good at (tick the box):

   ☐ talking   ☐ making people feel comfortable

   ☐ listening   ☐ remembering birthdays

   ☐ making people laugh   ☐ giving time to charity

   ☐ including people   ☐ helping other people

Dear Diary...

Date: _____

Today's lesson title in SPHE was... _____

We learned about... _____

_____

One interesting topic we discussed was... _____

_____

Here is something new that I learned... _____

_____

I must remember to talk to my parents/guardians about... _____

Parent's/guardian's signature   My signature

_____

Any comments? _____

_____

Comments from teachers or parents/guardians can be written here but this does not have to be filled in every week.

lesson 16
Changes at adolescence

At the end of this lesson you will:

Know who to ask for help if you are having problems.

Understand the physical, social and psychological changes that take place during adolescence.

Understand the cause and effects of these changes.

Last week you completed your profile to see what makes you unique and different. This week you will do the same thing but you are going to fill it out as your eight-year-old self. This activity will make you realise how much you have grown and developed since then.

---

facebook   Search   Home   Profile   Find friends   Account ▼

Age: _____ eight _____

Hair colour: _____

Eye colour: _____

Favourite food: _____

Favourite movie: _____

Favourite subject: _____

Least favourite subject: _____

Hobbies: _____

The best day I ever had was: _____

Pet hates: _____

Ambition: _____

Changes at adolescence

Puberty occurs during adolescence. Adolescence simply means the teenage years when a child starts becoming an adult. During puberty, your body changes more quickly than any other time in your life so it can be scary. Everyone develops at different rates so don't be embarrassed if you think you are developing more quickly or at a slower rate than your friends. There is no timetable or schedule for when each change should occur, so stop worrying about why something hasn't happened yet! The changes that you can expect to happen can be divided into four groups:

1. Emotional changes

2. Mental changes

3. Social changes

4. Physical changes

It is important that you know about the changes that are going to happen to you. You also need to know about the changes that will happen to the opposite sex so that you can be sensitive to their feelings too.

Emotional changes

During puberty, hormones are produced to prepare your body for reproduction. These hormones can also cause changes to your emotions so you may find that sometimes you cannot control how you feel. As you get older the hormones will balance out and it will be easier to deal with your emotions. You will learn more about emotions in Lesson 21.

Make a list of the wide range of emotions that you may experience as a teenager. Each person in the class should name one emotion and add it to the list.

_____

_____

_____

_____

Mental changes

During adolescence, you begin to think more like an adult. As your mind develops, you can make more sense of things that you didn't understand as a child and you become more aware of other people's feelings. This change is more gradual so you might not notice it as much as other changes that occur during adolescence. Some adolescents will still act immaturely by being thoughtless or insensitive to other people. Every person's mind will develop at a different rate depending on their intelligence and experiences. Mental development is not something that just starts when you become a teenager and stops when you become an adult; it continues throughout your life.

Think of an example that shows how your mind has developed. For example, maybe you used to believe in the tooth fairy. Share your answer with the class.

Social changes

In your teenage years, you will find that you develop more meaningful relationships than you did as a child. For instance, you may find yourself more interested in having boyfriend/girlfriend relationships and your existing friendships might change. Your role in your family may also change. You may be given more responsibility, such as babysitting, or your parents may expect more of you, such as helping with chores.

Have your relationships with the following people changed recently?

	Yes	No
Parents		
Siblings		
Friends		
Boyfriends/girlfriends		

Physical changes

Your body must change from that of a child to that of an adult to allow reproduction to be possible when you are older. The physical changes that happen during puberty are the ones that you may be most conscious of. Your body will develop when it is ready, so do not worry if you are developing at a different rate to everyone else. Physical changes to your body during puberty can make you feel uncomfortable and embarrassed because you think that everyone notices. Remember that all your friends and other people your age are going through these changes as well and they probably feel the same way. One of the most common questions teenagers ask themselves during puberty is: 'Is this normal?' so here is a list of 'normal' changes you can expect to happen.

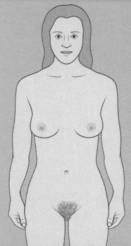

Boys	Girls
✿ Testicles increase in size and produce sperm	✿ Breasts develop
✿ Shoulders become wider and heavier	✿ Pelvic region widens and hips grow
✿ Muscle mass increases on shoulders, arms and legs	✿ Menstruation begins
✿ Increase in height	✿ Female reproductive organs grow
✿ Penis grows thicker and longer	✿ Pubic hair and underarm hair grow
✿ Pubic hair, underarm hair and facial hair grow	✿ Vaginal wall thickens and secretes moisture
✿ Voice deepens	✿ Acne or spots develop on the face, neck or other areas
✿ Acne or spots develop on face, neck or other areas	

There are lots of places where you can find out more about these changes and lots of people you can talk to about puberty. See the list below:

☆ **Parents** ☆ **Teachers** ☆ **School guidance counsellor** ☆ **Doctor**

These websites are particularly helpful:

 www.spunout.ie www.irishhealth.com www.b4udecide.ie

What are the four main types of changes experienced at adolescence?

Give one example of a change you have experienced for each type.

Type of change	Example from my experience

Dear Diary...

Date: _____

Today's lesson title in SPHE was... _____

We learned about... _____
_____

One interesting topic we discussed was... _____

Here is something new that I learned... _____
_____

I must remember to talk to my parents/guardians about... _____

Parent's/guardian's signature _____ My signature _____

Any comments? _____

Comments from teachers or parents/guardians can be written here but this <u>does not</u> have to be filled in every week.

lesson 17
Reproductive system 1

At the end of this lesson you will:

Have a clear understanding of the female reproductive system.

Understand the importance of the menstrual cycle in relation to conception.

Opening activity

Below is a word search containing ten words relating to the female reproductive system. It is a race to see who can find all ten words first.

d	r	a	d	f	g	j	l	o	v	c	s	w	v	f	r	w	a	m	n	u
m	h	s	a	d	t	g	j	k	y	i	e	a	o	x	q	e	v	e	z	a
o	d	e	f	h	t	u	i	p	q	e	f	g	v	m	b	w	q	n	v	r
e	q	f	t	s	a	v	j	a	l	d	s	e	t	u	b	v	s	o	m	y
s	b	x	d	f	g	e	n	m	l	t	d	w	e	y	t	g	j	p	b	v
t	q	f	r	h	i	i	u	f	d	c	g	s	f	e	s	a	f	a	t	w
r	e	f	g	t	g	j	l	w	r	e	g	g	q	a	w	e	d	u	f	e
o	g	f	a	a	b	t	s	f	j	u	s	a	e	g	j	v	a	s	b	n
g	z	e	v	b	e	q	d	n	k	d	a	x	g	u	n	s	r	e	h	p
e	w	f	g	j	l	t	c	e	r	v	i	x	v	b	n	k	g	u	g	e
n	b	g	a	q	p	i	u	j	o	f	v	j	s	t	r	b	v	a	p	r
u	t	j	u	f	d	r	b	n	u	o	v	u	l	a	t	i	o	n	w	i
w	f	v	b	r	e	a	s	t	s	t	h	s	v	r	h	k	p	o	b	o
e	f	g	h	k	l	u	f	s	j	b	d	o	v	a	r	y	t	v	w	d

The female reproductive system

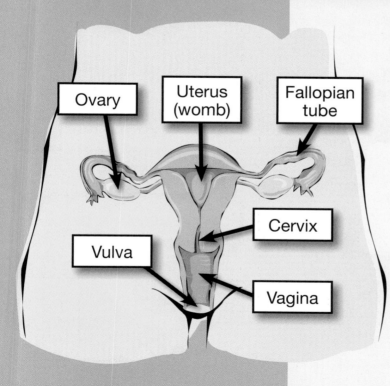

Ovary

Uterus (womb)

Fallopian tube

Cervix

Vulva

Vagina

☆ The vulva is at the opening of the vagina. It is the only part of the female reproductive organs visible on the outside – the rest are inside the body. The vagina is a muscular tube.

☆ The vagina leads to the cervix or the neck of the uterus (womb).

☆ The uterus is a hollow organ with muscular walls, which allow it to stretch to hold a baby. It is about the same size as a pear.

☆ Two fallopian tubes on either side of the womb connect the womb to the ovaries.

☆ The ovaries produce hormones such as oestrogen and progesterone; these hormones control sexual development, menstruation and pregnancy.

The menstrual cycle

- ☆ Once every month, hormones cause an egg (or ovum) to be produced and released from the ovaries. This is called ovulation.

- ☆ The egg released by the ovaries travels slowly down the fallopian tubes towards the womb.

- ☆ If this egg is fertilised by a sperm it will turn into a baby. The womb begins to prepare for a baby by developing a thick lining of blood and tissue on its inner walls. This lining will help to protect the baby as it grows.

- ☆ If the egg is not fertilised, the lining breaks down and both the egg and the lining leave the womb through the cervix and vagina. This is called menstruation, or a period. The bleeding time varies, lasting between three and seven days. Usually, the whole process begins again about 28 days later. This process is called the menstrual cycle.

During puberty the menstrual cycle can be very irregular, but will become more regular over time. Menstruation starts around the age of 12 but this can vary depending on body shape, size and hormones. There is no way of telling when a girl is going to have her first period, so she should always keep sanitary protection in her bag just in case. Nobody else will know when a girl is having her period unless she chooses to tell them. Menstruation is one of the first steps a girl's body takes to change from a girl to a woman, because it means she can now physically conceive and bear a child. Menstruation stops during the menopause.

The menopause

The menopause usually happens between the ages of 45 to 55. Periods may become quite irregular before they stop altogether. During menopause less oestrogen and other hormones are produced. The imbalance of hormones can make the woman quite emotional and she may experience 'hot flushes' (getting very hot or sweaty). Usually, after the menopause a woman cannot get pregnant naturally.

Take a few minutes to study the female reproductive system and then try to label the blank diagram on the right without looking back.

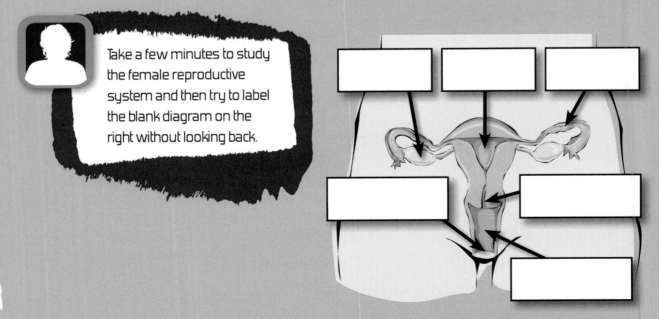

Answer true or false to the following statements.	True	False
1. Menstruation always begins at the age of 12.		
2. An egg or ovum is released from the ovaries every month.		
3. An unfertilised egg can still develop into a baby.		
4. The uterus has two fallopian tubes.		
5. Menstruation will continue for the rest of the woman's life.		
6. The uterus develops a lining of blood and tissue to prepare for a fertilised egg.		
7. The uterus is also known as the ovaries.		

Answer the following questions.

1. What is another name for an ovum?

2. What is another name for the womb?

3. What is the function of the thick layer of blood and tissue that lines the uterus every month?

4. Name two hormones produced in the ovaries.

5. How long does the menstrual cycle usually last?

Dear Diary...

Date: _____

Today's lesson title in SPHE was... _____

We learned about... _____
_____

One interesting topic we discussed was... _____
_____

Here is something new that I learned... _____
_____

I must remember to talk to my parents/guardians about... _____

Parent's/guardian's signature _____   My signature _____

Any comments? _____

Comments from teachers or parents/guardians can be written here but this does not have to be filled in every week.

lesson 18
Reproductive system 2

At the end of this lesson you will:

Have a clear understanding of the male reproductive system.

Have a clear understanding of intercourse and conception.

In groups of four, complete the following exercise. One person will need a pen and paper. The teacher will call out five letters, and you have two minutes to come up with as many words as you can beginning with each letter. Each word must be a male body part (no slang allowed). For example if the teacher says 'L', you could answer lips, legs, lungs. The group with the most correct words wins.

The male reproductive system

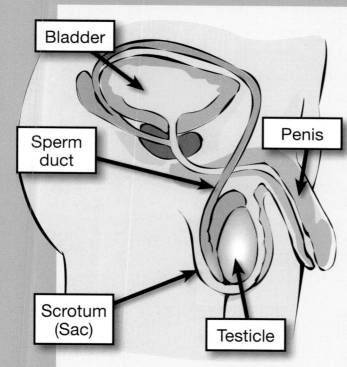

Bladder

Sperm duct

Penis

Scrotum (Sac)

Testicle

- ✡ The penis and scrotum (or sac) are visible outside the body.

- ✡ The scrotum is a loose pouch of skin that contains the testes (two testicles).

- ✡ The testes produce sperm and the sperm travels through a sperm duct inside the body to the penis.

- ✡ The testes also produce testosterone, a hormone that controls male sexual development.

- ✡ The production of testosterone during puberty causes the penis to grow larger.

- ✡ During puberty, the testes start producing sperm, which means that the boy can now physically father a child.

- ✡ Adolescent boys may begin to experience erections. These are caused by blood rushing into the penis and making it become erect or 'hard'. Usually this happens when a boy is sexually aroused, but during puberty it can happen at other times too and can be embarrassing. Don't worry – this phase won't last too long.

- ✡ Boys may also start having 'wet' dreams. This means that they 'come' or ejaculate during their sleep, releasing sperm in a fluid called semen. This is entirely normal. A boy doesn't have to ejaculate every time that he has an erection.

- ✡ The foreskin is the skin covering the end of the penis.

- ✡ Underneath the foreskin are glands that secrete smegma. This is a white and creamy discharge that helps the skin slide back and forth. All males are born with a foreskin, but some are circumcised, which means the foreskin has been removed surgically.

Answer true or false to the following statements.

		True	False
1.	The testes produce sperm.		
2.	Testosterone is a hormone that causes the penis to grow.		
3.	A rush of semen to the penis causes an erection.		
4.	The testes are contained in the scrotum outside the body.		
5.	The sac is another name for the scrotum.		
6.	Erections only occur when a boy is aroused.		

Fertilisation and conception

During sexual intercourse (sex), the man's penis enters the woman's vagina. When the man ejaculates, semen is released into the vagina. The man's sperm then swims up into the woman's uterus and into the fallopian tube. Fertilisation occurs if the man's sperm and the woman's egg meet in this tube. The father's sperm goes to the centre of the mother's egg and joins with it. The new cell that results begins to divide and subdivide. After seven to ten days, the fertilised egg moves down the tube into the mother's uterus. It is growing all the time. The cells nestle in the lining of the uterus; this is called implantation. This whole process is called conception and fertilisation. The cells develop into a baby over the next 40 weeks. The mother will probably realise she is pregnant when her next period does not come, usually around 14 days after fertilisation.

Take a few minutes to study the male reproductive system. Then label the blank diagram on the right without looking back.

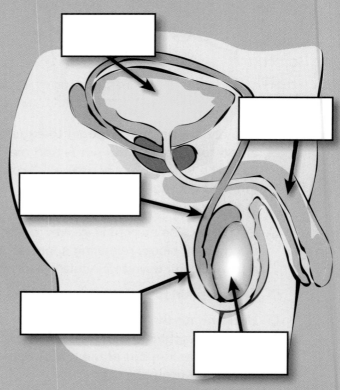

Answer the following questions.

1. Name a hormone which is responsible for male sexual development.

2. What is the function of the testes?

3. Explain what an erection is.

4. What is fertilisation?

5. How long does pregnancy last?

Dear Diary...

Date: _____

Today's lesson title in SPHE was... _____

We learned about... _____
_____

One interesting topic we discussed was... _____
_____

Here is something new that I learned... _____
_____

I must remember to talk to my parents/guardians about... _____
_____
_____

Parent's/guardian's signature _____   My signature _____

Any comments? _____
_____
_____

Comments from teachers or parents/guardians can be written here but this does not have to be filled in every week.

lesson 19
Images of males and females

At the end of this lesson you will:

Be aware of stereotyping and its influence on your attitudes and behaviour.

Understand how gender stereotyping affects your lifestyle.

Opening activity

Your teacher will put up an **Agree** and a **Disagree** sign in two corners of the classroom. Stand at the right place in the classroom according to whether you agree or disagree with the following statements.

1. Women are better than men at staying at home and minding the kids.
2. Girls should be able to ask guys out.
3. Boys' sports are really more important than girls' sports.
4. Men make good secretaries and nurses.
5. Boys should hide their feelings if at all possible.
6. If a husband and wife both work, they should both help with the cooking and cleaning at home.
7. Girls have more feelings than boys.
8. Men are better drivers than women.
9. The husband should have the final say.
10. It's just as OK for men to cry as for women.
11. Girls should help pay for dates.
12. Education is more important for boys than for girls.
13. Women make good construction workers and engineers.
14. Boys should learn how to cook, sew, clean the house and do laundry.

Stereotyping

Stereotyping means putting people into a category or presuming certain groups of people are all alike. People have learned not to stereotype as much as they used to. For example, at the beginning of the twentieth century, women were not allowed to vote or go to university because they were not thought to be as clever as men. If men cared for the children or did housework, they were thought to be weak or soft. We have come a long way since then, but stereotyping still exists, especially the stereotyping of males and females. This is called gender stereotyping. Gender stereotyping leads us to believe certain **traits** are male or female.

Trait

A trait is a mannerism or characteristic of a person.

Below is a list of traits. In pairs, decide whether you would consider the trait to be masculine or feminine. Can you think of more masculine or feminine traits to add to the list?

Trait	Masculine	Feminine
Very private or guarded about personal feelings		
Caring/loving		
Emotional		
Violent/aggressive		
Gossipmonger (a person who gossips a lot)		
Tough		

Gender learning

From the day you were born, you were probably treated differently because of your gender. For example, girls are often dressed in pink and boys in blue. This has been going on all through your life, probably without you even noticing. For hundreds of years people have discussed whether males and females are different because of nature (their genetic makeup) or nurture (the way they are raised and treated). One example of gender learning occurring at a young age is the types of toys you were given to play with. The next activity explores this issue.

As a group, draw up a list of toys that girls/boys are usually given to play with. Then discuss what the child is subconsciously learning.

Boys' toys	What are they learning?
Action Man	Boys should be tough and strong

Girls' toys	What are they learning?
Barbie	Girls should be thin, beautiful and enjoy shopping

Effects of stereotyping

Stereotypes are often exaggerated images of certain groups of people and a lot of the time are completely untrue. If we continually stereotype males and females or other groups of people we are then judging people before we even know them. This is not a good way to form any type of friendship or relationship. It is very important to note that while men and women are certainly different, they are also equal. Because of gender stereotyping, girls and boys are often expected to behave or act in a certain way.

You may find that you are treated differently than your brothers or sisters because of your sex. Discuss the advantages and disadvantages of being a boy or a girl.

1. If you were born a member of the opposite sex, what opportunities would you have that you feel you don't have right now?

_____

_____

_____

2. Some careers are seen as 'male careers' or 'female careers', even though men and women could both be good at that particular job. Make a list of careers that you wouldn't expect men/women to typically work at.

I wouldn't normally expect to see a man working as a...

_____

_____

I wouldn't normally expect to see a woman working as a...

_____

_____

Interview your parents/ guardians (tell them about today's lesson first). Ask the following questions:

1. How were males and females treated differently in your family?

_____

_____

_____

2. Were boys and girls treated differently because of their gender when you went to school?

_____

_____

_____

3. What do you think are some advantages of being a male/female?

_____

_____

_____

Dear Diary...

Date: _____

Today's lesson title in SPHE was... _____

We learned about... _____

_____

One interesting topic we discussed was... _____

_____

Here is something new that I learned... _____

_____

_____

I must remember to talk to my parents/guardians about... _____

_____

Parent's/guardian's signature   My signature

_____

Any comments? _____

_____

Comments from teachers or parents/guardians can be written here but this <u>does not</u> have to be filled in every week.

lesson 20
Respecting myself and others

At the end of this lesson you will:

Recognise the importance of respecting other people and yourself.

Understand what is meant by sexuality.

ReSPECt

Understand the importance of respecting other peoples' sexuality.

Everyone sits in a circle. One person stands in the middle and does not have a chair. The person in the middle asks a question, and whoever answers 'yes' has to get up and change chairs with someone else. The person in the middle has to try and get a chair. As you arrange the chairs in the classroom into a circle, think of some questions you can use for this game. For example:

★ Have you ever been to Cork?

★ Have you ever fallen off a bicycle?

★ Have you ever climbed the Bluestack Mountains?

Respecting yourself and others

It's probably not something you think about very often, but respecting yourself is really important. Learning to respect yourself and other people is a vital part of growing up and becoming an adult.

Respecting yourself

Everyone has to learn to respect himself or herself. We can respect our bodies by:

★ **Not smoking or using drugs.**

★ **Not eating the wrong type of food.**

★ **Keeping fit.**

★ **Getting enough sleep.**

★ **Treating any illness we might have.**

★ **Maintaining good personal hygiene and good grooming.**

Write a list of the things you do that show that you respect your body. For example, 'I choose not to smoke'.

_____

_____

_____

_____

_____

_____

Respecting others

Respecting others is just as important as respecting yourself. There are many people in society who do not get the respect they deserve such as Travellers, people with disabilities and gay people. All people are equal and should be treated equally. If we treat someone differently because of his or her race, culture or ability it is called discrimination. You can show respect for other people by:

- Listening to them.
- Being kind.
- Not making fun of their feelings or opinions.
- Not betraying their secrets.

- Letting them have privacy.
- Not making them do things they don't want to do.
- Not being mean or making them feel bad.

If you don't show respect for other people, soon people will lose respect for you and you will not have many real friends. Always ask yourself how would you feel about being treated a particular way before you treat someone else like that.

In groups of four, discuss the following. Write down the main points.

How can you show respect for:

1. Parents

_____

_____

_____

_____

2. The elderly

_____

_____

_____

_____

3. People with a disability

_____

_____

_____

_____

Sex and sexuality

It is important to understand that **sex** and **sexuality** are two different things.

Sexual orientation

Part of your sexuality is your sexual orientation. This means whether you fancy boys or girls, or if you fancy both. During your teenage years, you might feel unsure about your sexuality or who you find attractive. 'Homosexual' or 'gay' is the term used to describe people who are attracted to people of the same sex. 'Heterosexual' or 'straight' refers to people who are attracted to the opposite sex. Bisexual people are attracted to both sexes.

You don't have to tell your friends anything about your sexuality or who you fancy unless you want to, but remember it does help to talk.

Whatever a person's sexual orientation is, remember it is only one part of a person's identity. Nobody should be discriminated against because of their sexuality.

Sex

Sex refers to whether a person is male or female. Sex is also commonly used as an abbreviation to refer to sexual intercourse.

Sexuality

Sexuality is about how you think, act and feel. Your sexuality depends on your body image, gender, identity, gender roles and sexual orientation. It includes attitudes, values, knowledge and behaviours.

Discuss some of the ways that people are discriminated against because of their sexuality.
Do not use offensive terms when discussing sexuality - only use the following words:

- ☆ Gay
- ☆ Lesbian
- ☆ Homosexual
- ☆ Straight
- ☆ Bisexual
- ☆ Heterosexual

Write two ways that you can show respect for the sexual orientation of your friends/peers.

_____

_____

_____

_____

You will learn more about sexuality in Second and Third Year. In the meantime you can find out more information from the site below.

 BeLonG To (www.belongto.org) is an organisation for Lesbian, Gay, Bisexual and Transgendered (LGBT) young people, aged between 14 and 23.

Below are some questions to help you think about your own sexuality. You may like to discuss some of these questions with a parent or guardian. You do not need to write the answers here but you could write them somewhere private.

1. The things I like about being male/female are...

2. The things I don't like about being male/female are...

3. Am I respectful to other people's sexuality? (Do I act differently towards people who have a different sexual orientation or a different attitude to sex than me?)

Dear Diary...

Date: _____

Today's lesson title in SPHE was... _____

We learned about... _____

One interesting topic we discussed was... _____

Here is something new that I learned... _____

I must remember to talk to my parents/guardians about... _____

Parent's/guardian's signature _____   My signature _____

Any comments? _____

Comments from teachers or parents/guardians can be written here but this <u>does not</u> have to be filled in every week.

module 7
Emotional health

This module focuses on feelings – where they come from and what effect they have. It encourages students to recognise their own feelings, a basic element of good mental health.

At the end of this module you will:

- Be aware of common emotions and associated words used to express them.

- Have explored your own emotional responses, and those of others around you.

- Be aware of the appropriate ways of expressing your emotions.

lesson 21
Recognising and respecting my feelings and those of others

At the end of this lesson you will:

Have developed skills for expressing your emotions.

Be able to identify and label common emotions.

Know how to express emotions in the right way.

Be more conscious of the feelings of others.

The teacher will write down a particular feeling or emotion and ask one student to express it to the class. The student can do this in two ways:

✪ by using body language or facial expressions

✪ by describing a situation where they might feel that emotion.

Whoever guesses correctly takes the next turn.

Expressing emotions

Emotion is the movement of feelings. You can experience emotion consciously – for example you can feel sad, happy or excited. You can also feel emotion physically – you may be shaking with nerves. Children usually let their emotions flow freely, but as we grow older we are expected to control our feelings and emotions and express them in the right way. Sometimes we deny our feelings or squash them down. Doing this may lead to stress or poor mental health.

1. Can you think of other examples of how people experience their emotions physically?

2. Give examples of how children freely express their emotions. Would it be appropriate for adults to express their emotions this way?

3. What feelings to people tend to deny or suppress?

Below are common **emoticons** that you use on your phone or in an email. In pairs, write one emotion that you think each symbol represents.

Emoticons
Emoticons are facial expressions shown by punctuation and letters or using pictures. They are used to express a writer's mood. They are used in text messages and online messaging.

In a group, write a list of emotions that you might feel in each of the following situations:

1. You have been called to the principal's office.

2. You have won €200 in a school raffle.

3. You have a huge spot on your nose and get a terrible haircut the day of the school disco.

4. You are playing in a football final and get taken off the pitch after only 20 minutes.

5. You arrange to meet a boy/girl at the cinema and he/she doesn't turn up.

6. The basketball coach tells you that you have won player of the year.

7. As you are taking out your books, your baby brother's teddy bear falls out of your schoolbag and everybody laughs.

8. You went to every training session this year but still didn't get picked for the school basketball team.

9. The girl/boy you have fancied for ages asks you out.

10. You spend ages getting ready to go out. When you are finally ready, you come downstairs and your older brother laughs saying, 'Look at the state of you'.

Describing your feelings

It is important that you are able to describe your feelings and that you do not blame somebody else for how you feel. This is of particular importance in situations of conflict. Follow these steps to help you describe your feelings.

- ✿ **Name the feeling, for example: 'I feel angry.'**

- ✿ **Try to understand why you feel the way you do – sometimes you may not know why you feel that way.**

- ✿ **Use 'I' statements to describe your feelings, for example: 'I feel sad/angry/ disappointed', not 'You are horrible' or 'You don't understand what it's like'.**

- ✿ **Speak in the present, because feelings can change. Instead of 'You're always mean to me', say 'I feel upset because what you said embarrassed me'.**

Practise these steps for describing your emotions by acting out the following role-plays in groups of two.

Role-play 1

Joe lent Craig some money six weeks ago and told him he needed it back soon to buy his girlfriend a birthday present. He has not asked for the money back but knows that Craig started a new part-time job three weeks ago and feels he should now have the cash to repay him. Joe bumps into Craig in the shopping centre and Craig shows him the new phone he just bought.

Act out the conversation between Joe and Craig.

Role-play 2

Amanda has known Joanne since Third Class. She has covered for Joanne several times, saying that they are having a sleepover when in fact Joanne has been staying with her boyfriend. Yesterday Joanne's mother gave out to Amanda and called her a liar. Joanne says she just wants her to cover for her one more time so that she can go to a concert. Amanda no longer wants to lie and feels used in this situation.

Act out the conversation between Amanda and Joanne.

Role-play 3

John has always been a good employee and has enjoyed working as an assistant in his local shop. He is always on time and is polite to the customers. Lately his boss, whom he used to get on well with, has been giving out to John a lot. He keeps making remarks suggesting that John is not working hard enough and that he is not doing his job well. John feels hurt and annoyed by this because he does not know what he has done wrong. He is now considering leaving the job.

Act out the conversation between John and his boss.

Next week you will be doing a project in class called 'My hero'. You will be writing a profile about a person you admire or who inspires you, then the other students will be reading what you write. Gather information on one of your heroes. This can include photos, details about their life or information about their talents. Remember your hero can be someone you know: heroes do not only appear in magazines.

1. Identify a song that makes you feel happy.

2. Name a movie that makes you feel sad.

3. Which colours make you feel relaxed?

4. Describe a time when you were a child and you were really excited about something.

Dear Diary...

Date: _____

Today's lesson title in SPHE was... _____

We learned about... _____

One interesting topic we discussed was... _____

Here is something new that I learned... _____

I must remember to talk to my parents/guardians about... _____

Parent's/guardian's signature _____   My signature _____

Any comments? _____

Comments from teachers or parents/guardians can be written here but this <u>does not</u> have to be filled in every week.

module 8
Influences and decisions

In this module you will examine the ways in which you are influenced, without even being conscious of it. Being aware of these influences is the first step in developing the critical skills needed for good decision-making.

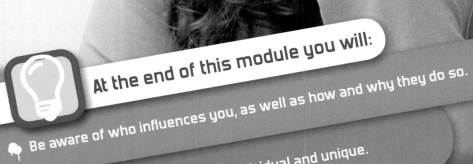

At the end of this module you will:

- Be aware of who influences you, as well as how and why they do so.

- Respect how each person is individual and unique.

lesson 22
My heroes

At the end of this lesson you will:

Be able to appreciate how everyone is an individual and different.

Have identified people who have a big influence in your life.

Have explored how these people influence you.

Opening activity

In groups of five, play this 20 questions game. One student thinks of a character from a TV show. The others have to guess who it is by asking no more than 20 questions to which the answer can only be yes or no.

Me versus TV

Choose a TV character from a show you like. The character should be the same sex and around the same age as you. Using the following table, compare your lives. Use colours and symbols or pictures as well as words.

Me	TV character
Draw a picture of you	*Draw a picture of the TV character*
My school life	His/her school life
My social life	His/her social life
My friends	His/her friends
My family	His/her family

Are the teenage characters you see on television like teenagers in real life? Do they influence how you act or behave? Who else influences how you act or behave?

My Hero

Name: Paula O'Driscoll

Other names: Ma, Mammy, Mum

Date of birth: She won't tell me.

Nationality: Irish

Talents: Makes the best chicken curry ever, always makes me laugh, knows when to leave me alone, is a great listener, patient, a good tennis player, and never gives up

About her: I picked my mother as my hero because she is the person I admire most in the world. She is mother to me and my two brothers. She never loses her patience with me (well, almost never), even though I know she is wrecked when she comes home from work. She held our family together after my Dad died three years ago. Even though I know she is sad and she misses him loads, she can always cheer me up. I can talk to her about anything.

What has she taught me? To enjoy life. To show respect for other people. That it is OK to be sad sometimes.

What I would like to say to her: Thank you. I know I don't say it enough and I know I complain about not being allowed to do what I want all the time, but thank you for being the best mammy a boy could wish for.

My Hero

Name: Katie Taylor

Other names: None

Date of birth: 2 June, 1986

Nationality: Irish

Talents: Boxing champion, friendly, humble

About her: Katie Taylor made Irish boxing history at only 18. In May 2005 she became the first Irish woman to win a gold medal at the Senior European Boxing Championships. As World Boxing Champion 2008 and 2007, Triple European Boxing Champion and captain of the Irish female football team, she represents Ireland at the highest levels in both boxing and football. I picked her as my hero because she proves that women can succeed in sports that are considered to be 'men's sports' and she never gave up when people put her down or told her that she shouldn't be boxing.

What has she taught me? She has taught me to follow my dreams and the importance of good sportsmanship.

What I would like to say to her: Katie, you make me proud to be Irish, you have natural talent and work extremely hard. You have inspired me to keep going with my favourite sport, rugby. Best of luck in your next fight!

My Hero

Name: Arsène Wenger

Other names: Le Professeur, Master Gunner

Date of birth: 22 October, 1949

Nationality: French

Talents: Excellent manager, an ability to motivate players, a great understanding of sports psychology

About him: He has had an amazing career managing soccer teams: 1996–present – manager of Arsenal; 1995–96 – head coach of Grampus Eight, Japan; 1987–94 head coach of Monaco; 1984 head coach of Nancy, France; 1983 – assistant coach of Cannes, France; 1981 – youth coach of Strasbourg, France. Some of his honours include: Premiership titles in 1998, 2002 and 2004; FA Cup wins – 1998; 2002; 2003 (all with Arsenal).

What has he taught me? To strive for success always, no matter what gets in the way.

What I would like to say to him: Congratulations on managing one of the most successful clubs and for spotting the talent in new players.

Fill in the following details on your chosen hero, adding a photo if you have one.

Insert photo here

My Hero

Name: _____

Other names: _____

Date of birth: _____

Nationality: _____

Talents: _____

_____

About him/her: _____

_____

_____

What has he/she taught me? _____

_____

_____

What I would like to say to him/her: _____

_____

_____

Make a list of the people that you influence.

How do you influence them?

Dear Diary...

Date: _____

Today's lesson title in SPHE was... _____

_____

We learned about... _____

_____

_____

One interesting topic we discussed was... _____

_____

_____

Here is something new that I learned... _____

_____

_____

I must remember to talk to my parents/guardians about... _____

_____

_____

_____

Parent's/guardian's signature _____   My signature _____

_____

Any comments? _____

_____

_____

Comments from teachers or parents/guardians can be written here but this <u>does not</u> have to be filled in every week.

module 9
Substance use

This module focuses on the place of drugs in everyday life and how they are used to treat and prevent illness. It also explores the misuse of drugs.

 At the end of this module you will:

• Have examined the place of medicines and drugs in human life.

• Be aware of how medicines and drugs can be misused.

• Understand what alcohol use means for personal health and social interaction.

• Have explored some of the reasons why people begin to smoke.

• Have examined ways of avoiding smoking.

lesson 23
Why drugs?

At the end of this lesson you will:

Understand the health and social implications of drug use.

Be aware of how medicine can be used correctly or misused.

Know where to get help if you or someone you know has a drug problem.

Have identified health implications of solvent abuse.

Understand the importance of medicine in our lives.

Write your thoughts about drugs on the 'Word Wall' below. Use colours, symbols and pictures as well as words.

Drugs

Medicine

Medicine is extremely important to us. It helps us to live longer and to get better more quickly when we are sick. Medicine is also important for people with a disease or an illness – it can help them to lead a normal life.

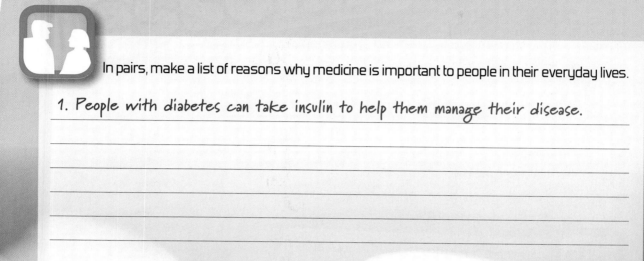

In pairs, make a list of reasons why medicine is important to people in their everyday lives.

1. People with diabetes can take insulin to help them manage their disease.

_____

_____

_____

_____

_____

_____

_____

About drug abuse

✿ Drug abuse is the misuse of drugs. This means not using them as they are meant to be used, for example to treat pain or illness.

✿ Drug abuse may involve legal or illegal drugs.

✿ A person who misuses drugs is a drug abuser.

✿ Drug abusers do not abuse drugs; they abuse their bodies with drugs.

✿ A drug is a mind- or body-altering substance. This means it may change the way you feel, think, act or behave.

✿ Some drugs are more addictive than others and some people are more likely to become addicts than others.

Working in pairs, make a list of all the drugs you know.
State whether they are legal or illegal drugs.

What is a drug addict?

If a drug abuser becomes dependent on drugs, meaning they cannot live a normal life without drugs, then they become a drug addict. There are two types of dependence – psychological dependence and physical dependence. Psychological dependence is when the person depends on the drugs to make them feel better or even just to feel normal. Physical dependence is when the drug addict is so used to having the drug in their body that when they don't have it, their body will go into 'shock' or withdrawal. Withdrawal from each drug is different but symptoms may include nausea, pains, sickness, anxiety or aggression.

 Are there many drug addicts in your area or in the towns near where you live?

Misuse
Misuse is using something in the wrong way or for the wrong purpose for which it was intended.

Drug misuse in teenagers

Most people who **misuse** drugs start experimenting with drugs when they are teenagers. Teenagers often start by misusing solvents such as glue or aerosols as they are very easy to get. Then they often move on to illegal drugs.

Drug
A chemical substance that alters the body or mind.

 Do you think solvent misuse is common among teenagers? Why? What are the dangers of using solvents?

We will now explore drug use in teenagers. Answer the questions that follow.

1. How did Daryl get into drugs?

2. What problems were caused by Daryl's drug use?

3. What help did Daryl seek?

In groups of four, come up with a list of reasons why teenagers use drugs. You know the answers better than anyone because you are teenagers. There is one on the list already. Present your findings to the class.

1. Teenagers are naturally curious and may want to experiment with drugs to see what they are like.

If you or someone you know needs help with a drug problem, the following website can help: *www.drugs.ie* offers drug and alcohol information and support for teenagers and their parents and gives details of where to find help.

1. Write in your own words why medicine is so important.

_____

2. What is a drug?

_____

3. What are the two types of drug dependence? Explain what each means.

_____

_____

4. Why do drug addicts get withdrawal symptoms?

_____

5. In your opinion, what is the main reason that teenagers use drugs?

_____

Dear Diary...

Date: _____

Today's lesson title in SPHE was... _____
_____

We learned about... _____
_____
_____

One interesting topic we discussed was... _____
_____
_____

Here is something new that I learned... _____
_____
_____

I must remember to talk to my parents/guardians about... _____
_____
_____
_____

Parent's/guardian's signature _____   My signature _____
_____

Any comments? _____
_____
_____

Comments from teachers or parents/guardians can be written here but this <u>does not</u> have to be filled in every week.

lesson 24
Alcohol

At the end of this lesson you will:

Have explored the reasons why people drink alcohol.

Understand how alcohol abuse affects society and people's health.

Have examined the use of alcohol in Irish society.

Know where to get help if you or someone you know has an alcohol problem.

Write your thoughts about alcohol on the 'Word Wall' below. Use colours, symbols and pictures as well as words.

ALCOHOL

Responsible drinking

Alcohol is a drug that can be used sensibly and responsibly. However, it can also be used irresponsibly. Adults may choose to drink socially, with friends, with a meal or at a social occasion. A responsible drinker:

- ✩ knows when to stop drinking
- ✩ eats a meal while, or before, drinking alcohol
- ✩ does not drink and drive
- ✩ does not drink every day
- ✩ does not need to drink to have a good time.

As a class discuss the following:

Why do some people choose not to drink alcohol? Irish adults are among the highest consumers of alcohol in the EU. They drink about 20 per cent more than the average European. We often hear about Irish teenagers drinking too much, but do you think that Irish adults drink too much?

Binge drinking

This is the practice of drinking large amounts of alcohol at one time with the aim of getting drunk.

Facts about alcohol

- ✩ Alcohol can destroy brain tissue, which cannot be replaced.
- ✩ Between 61,000 and 104,000 children aged under 15 in Ireland are estimated to be living with parents who misuse alcohol.
- ✩ Alcohol has a lot of calories, but no nutrients.
- ✩ According to studies, more Irish girls than boys binge drink.
- ✩ Heart disease and liver disease can be caused by alcohol.
- ✩ Drinking alcohol while pregnant can damage the unborn baby.
- ✩ Alcohol lowers inhibitions, making people more likely to do things they would not normally do. Studies show that teenagers who have set limits on their sexual activity often go further than they intend to when under the influence of alcohol.
- ✩ Approximately 120 people are killed each year in alcohol-related crashes.

Alcohol quiz

1. What is the legal age to buy alcohol in Ireland? _____

2. Is alcohol a drug? _____

3. Is alcoholism a disease? _____

4. Can men 'hold their drink' better than women? _____

5. A blackout is when you pass out from drinking too much alcohol. True or false? _____

6. Drinking coffee or having a cold shower will sober you up. True or false? _____

Part 1

Find a TV or radio ad about underage drinking, then answer the following questions.

1. What message is the ad trying to convey?

    _____

2. Do you think the ad is effective? Why/why not?

    _____

3. Do you think underage drinking is a problem in your area?

    _____

Part 2

In groups of four, complete the table below. One example has already been done for you.

Why do young people drink?	What can be done to change this?
Boredom	Take up a hobby like learning guitar, join a club, volunteer, get a part-time job.

For more information on alcohol or for advice on where to get help if you or someone you know has a problem, check out the following websites. The contact details are at the back of the book.

    www.checkyourself.org   www.spunout.ie   www.barnardos.ie

Find out the price of the following in your local pub (ask an adult or check the price list displayed near the door):

⭐ a pint of beer   ⭐ a glass of wine   ⭐ a vodka and coke.

If you drank eight pints of beer every week for a year, how much would that cost?

Write about your attitude to alcohol. Here are some hints to get you started:

⭐ do you think it is a good or bad thing?

⭐ do you think it is often misused?

⭐ do you intend to drink responsibly?

_____

_____

_____

_____

_____

_____

_____

_____

Dear Diary...

Date: _____

Today's lesson title in SPHE was... _____

We learned about... _____

_____

One interesting topic we discussed was... _____

Here is something new that I learned... _____

_____

I must remember to talk to my parents/guardians about... _____

Parent's/guardian's signature _____   My signature _____

Any comments? _____

Comments from teachers or parents/guardians can be written here but this does not have to be filled in every week.

lesson 25
Smoking

At the end of this lesson you will:

Have examined the reasons why young people start smoking.

Know where to get help to give up smoking.

Have explored how smoking affects society and your health.

In the box below draw a quick diagram of a human body. Then mark with an X any area of the body that can be affected by smoking.

Getting addicted

Nobody has their first cigarette and thinks, 'Mmmm, this is lovely, I think I'll keep smoking for the rest of my life'. Most people actually feel sick when they have their first cigarette, because they are putting poison into their body. But they persist until they 'get used' to the taste. Usually they will start off with an odd cigarette, or sharing packets with friends. Then they start buying their own and gradually start smoking more and more. When teenagers start smoking they always think, 'I could give up any time I like – I am not addicted'. But they keep smoking and they become addicted. Lots of people say they are 'social smokers', so let's just see how social it is...

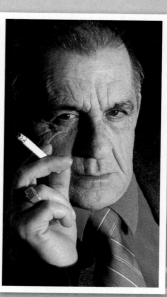

- ✪ **Your hair, breath and clothes stink of smoke.**
- ✪ **Your teeth go yellow.**
- ✪ **Your fingers and fingernails go yellow.**
- ✪ **You get more wrinkles, spots and dry skin.**
- ✪ **Every morning, you have to cough up phlegm, just so you can breathe properly.**
- ✪ **You are broke because so much of your money goes on buying cigarettes, so you don't have money to do things you enjoy.**
- ✪ **You get dirty looks from people if you smoke beside them.**
- ✪ **You usually have to smoke outside in the rain and cold.**

So, all in all, as you can see, the term 'social smoker' doesn't really make much sense.

In pairs, find out how much a packet of 20 cigarettes costs. If a person smokes 20 cigarettes a day, how much would they spend in:

(a) a week?

(b) a year?

(c) sixty years (assuming they start at 15 and die at 70)?

What would you do with that money?

What's in a cigarette?

Tobacco is made from the dried leaves of a plant called *Nicotiana tabacum*. When the leaves are burned, the smoke produced contains many harmful substances. Below are three of the most harmful.

Tar

Tar is a sticky, dark-brown substance. When someone smokes, they inhale (breathe in) tar into the lungs, lining the throat and lung tissues. Inhaling tar causes cancer and lung disease.

Nicotine

Nicotine is a stimulant drug and is very addictive. It narrows blood vessels in the body, which causes blood flow to slow down. This means your heart has to beat faster for your blood to circulate. If the heart constantly has to pump faster than it should, it will eventually tire or wear out.

Carbon monoxide

Carbon monoxide is a poisonous gas and is one of the gases that comes out of the exhaust of a car. Carbon monoxide robs the blood of oxygen, so that the organs in the body do not get the oxygen supply that they need. This can lead to heart disease and damage to other organs and blood vessels.

Risks of smoking

Seven thousand people die from the effects of tobacco each year in Ireland and thousands of others are ill because of tobacco-related diseases. Smoking can cause the following diseases:

The diseased lung of a smoker.

✿ cancer

✿ heart disease

✿ heart attack

✿ poor circulation

✿ bronchitis (tubes that lead to the lungs become inflamed and lined with mucus)

✿ emphysema (disease of the lungs).

In addition to these, if a pregnant woman smokes she can damage her unborn child.

Do you know anyone who has or had a smoking-related illness?

Giving up smoking

If you smoke, now is the time to give up. The longer you wait, the harder it is. Don't keep putting it off, set a date and stick to it. Here is a list of tips that may help you to give up.

☆ **Make a list of the reasons you want to give up, such as cost, health, not being fit enough to play sports, not wanting to smell like an ashtray.**

☆ **Tell people the day you are going to give up. They can support you and try to stop you having a cigarette if you think you want one.**

☆ **Get rid of all your lighters and cigarettes.**

☆ **Ask a pharmacist to recommend a suitable nicotine supplement for you – this will stop you craving (wanting) a cigarette and make it easier for you.**

☆ **If at first you don't succeed, try and try and try again!**

 To find out more advice, check out **www.quitwithhelp.ie** and **www.giveupsmoking.ie**

 It is not easy to give up smoking. Even though the nicotine is completely gone from the smoker's body a couple of days after they quit, the psychological dependence is much more difficult to deal with. Do you know anyone, maybe in your own family, who has tried to give up smoking?

 Most teenagers know the dangers of smoking but they still try it. Many become addicted. As a group come up with ideas as to what might stop a teenager from smoking. For example, you could appeal to their sense of vanity (smoking causes premature ageing, wrinkles, yellow teeth, bad breath...). Maybe your group could highlight the cost of smoking.

Design a leaflet/poster or an ad for TV based on your ideas.

Answer the following questions.

1. Name the plant tobacco comes from.

_____

2. What are the three most harmful substances in tobacco smoke?

(a) _____

(b) _____

(c) _____

3. What kind of drug is nicotine?

_____

4. Name four risks associated with smoking.

(a) _____

(b) _____

(c) _____

(d) _____

Dear Diary...

Date: _____

Today's lesson title in SPHE was... _____

We learned about... _____

_____

One interesting topic we discussed was... _____

Here is something new that I learned... _____

_____

I must remember to talk to my parents/guardians about... _____

_____

Parent's/guardian's signature _____   My signature _____

_____

Any comments? _____

_____

Comments from teachers or parents/guardians can be written here but this <u>does not</u> have to be filled in every week.

module 10
Personal safety

In this module you will revise road safety rules. Personal safety skills first learned in primary school are also revised and updated here.

 At the end of this module you will:

- Have examined ways of keeping safe.

- Be aware of the correct responses to a variety of threats to personal safety.

- Have practical knowledge of fire evacuation procedures.

- Have examined what hazards are involved in travelling to and from school.

lesson 26
Looking after myself

At the end of this lesson you will:

Be aware of the ways in which you can stay safe.

Know the evacuation rules in your school.

Have examined possible dangers in travelling to and from school.

Know how to react to threats to your personal safety.

I BELONG module 10 Personal safety

Opening activity

Complete this activity in pairs after you have read the fire evacuation notice in your classroom.

Pretend that you are an air steward and you have to give fire safety instructions to your partner. Start your presentation as follows: 'Good morning ladies and gentlemen, thank you for joining us in classroom 102. Before we start, there are a few safety procedures I would like to point out. As you can see, the exits are here, here and here. In the event of an emergency please. . .'

Fire safety

It is very unlikely that a fire will occur in your school but teachers and students have to be prepared for it just in case. Every classroom should have a fire evacuation plan.

Working in pairs, find the fire evacuation plan for your classroom and use it to answer the following questions.

1. How will you know if there is a fire? _____
   _____
   _____

2. What should you do with your schoolbooks and bags if an alarm sounds?
   _____
   _____

3. Where is the meeting point for your class? _____
   _____

4. What route and exit should you take to get to your meeting point?
   _____
   _____
   _____
   _____

Design a set of safety guidelines for students who travel to school:

✧ on foot
✧ by bus
✧ on a bicycle.

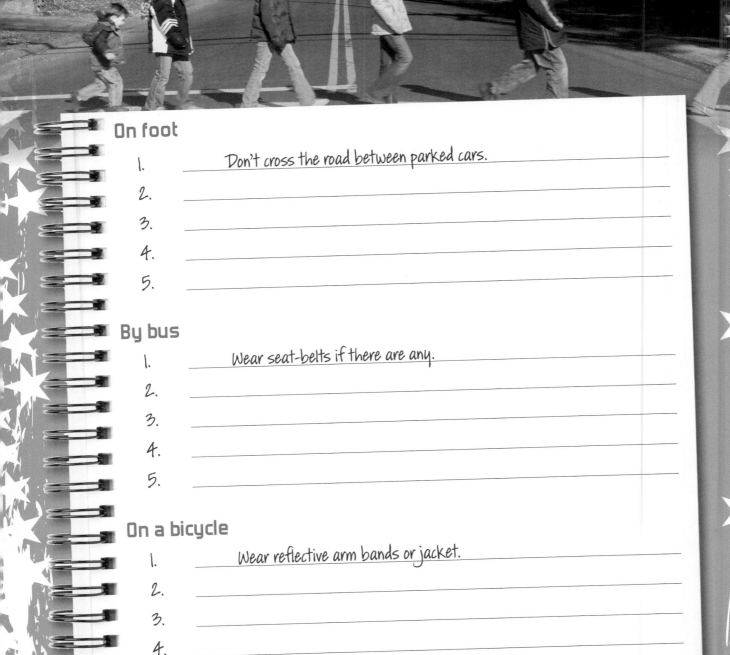

On foot

1. _Don't cross the road between parked cars._
2. _____
3. _____
4. _____
5. _____

By bus

1. _Wear seat-belts if there are any._
2. _____
3. _____
4. _____
5. _____

On a bicycle

1. _Wear reflective arm bands or jacket._
2. _____
3. _____
4. _____
5. _____

Design a road safety TV ad targeting teenagers travelling to school.

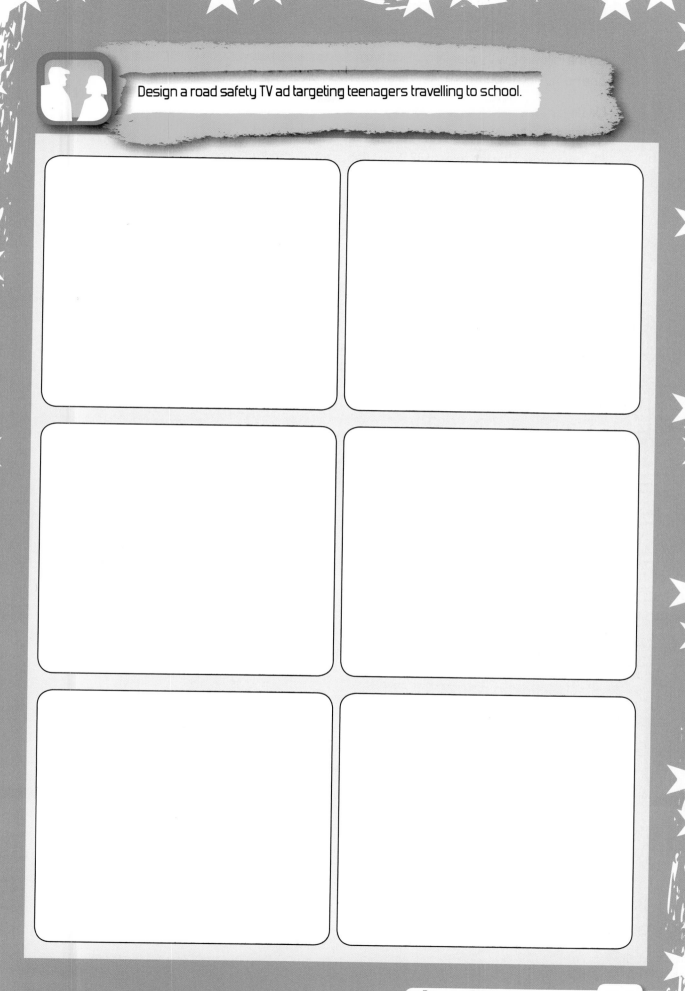

Discuss the following with your family and write the answers below. If you have more than one home you will have two sets of answers.

- ✪ Do you have a working smoke alarm? (One with no batteries or a broken one is no good!)

- ✪ Who checks the batteries in it? How often are they checked? (They should be checked once a week.)

- ✪ How will you exit your house if there is a fire upstairs?

- ✪ How will you exit if there is a fire downstairs?

- ✪ Where will your meeting point be if there is a fire?

- ✪ Who should you call if there is a fire? Write the numbers here.

- ✪ Emergency numbers _____

- ✪ After discussing these points with your family, you should decide on a date on which you will have a fire drill (in the next week).

Write the date here _____

Dear Diary...

Date: _____

Today's lesson title in SPHE was... _____

We learned about... _____
_____

One interesting topic we discussed was... _____

Here is something new that I learned... _____
_____

I must remember to talk to my parents/guardians about... _____

Parent's/guardian's signature _____   My signature _____

Any comments? _____
_____

Comments from teachers or parents/guardians can be written here but this does not have to be filled in every week.

Help agencies

The role of help agencies

Help agencies play a very important role in society. One of the reasons for this is that they make people aware of particular problems that exist, such as drug abuse. Some receive funding from the government; others receive no funding at all – they rely on donations and voluntary workers. Help agencies can be expensive to run, particularly if they have a website and a helpline. Staff must be trained, websites must be maintained, the help agency has to be advertised and research needs to be done. Many people need advice or reassurance and sometimes it is easier to talk to a stranger about a problem or to a person who understands what you are going through and is trained to deal with your problem.

Many help agencies offer some or all of the following services:

✪ **a website where you can access information**
✪ **free advice**
✪ **a helpline**
✪ **an online chat facility**
✪ **a free text facility.**

How to assist help agencies

Never 'prank call' a help agency. You are wasting their valuable time and a person who really needs their help might not be able to get through because of you. However if you have a problem or concern, do not hesitate to call. If you look at the website of any help agency you will often find a section that gives you details of how you can help raise much-needed funds. For example you could organise a sponsored silence, a walk, bungee jump or cake or book sale. You could also make an effort to support any activity in your school which is fundraising for a help agency.

List of help agencies

Abuse

www.childline.ie

Childline gives support to young people through a freephone 24-hour listening service and through its website. All calls are free of charge and confidential.

Freephone helpline: **1800 666 666**

Text support: text **list** to **50101** (This is an automated free text support service.)

www.ispcc.ie

Teenfocus is a support service to teenagers aged 13–18 who are having difficulties. It is run by the Irish Society for the Prevention of Cruelty to Children (ISPCC).

www.letsomeoneknow.ie

This is an Irish website for teenagers covering a range of different issues that are important in teenagers' lives.

www.teenline.ie

Teen-Line Ireland is a confidential helpline service for teenagers, dealing with any problems or worries they are experiencing.

Freephone helpline: **1800 833 634**

www.amen.ie

This site provides support for male victims of domestic abuse. It also offers help to their children.

www.womensaid.ie
This helps women and children who are suffering physical, mental/emotional, and/or sexual abuse in their homes.
Freephone helpline: **1800 341 900**

Addiction

National drugs and HIV helpline
This gives confidential support and information for drug users and those affected by HIV.
Freephone helpline: **1800 459 459**

www.drugs.ie
Provides information, support and counselling in relation to drugs, substance misuse or addiction.
Tel: **01 836 0911**

www.alcoholicsanonymous.ie
Alcoholics Anonymous is a fellowship of men and women who share their experience, strength and hope with each other in order to solve their common problem and help others to recover from alcoholism.
Email: **gso@alcoholicsanonymous.ie**
Tel: **01 453 8998**

www.al-anon-ireland.org
Alateen is for young people aged 12 to 20 who are affected by a problem drinker either at home or in their circle.
Email: **info@al-anon-ireland.org**
Tel: **01 873 2699**

www.na-ireland.org
Narcotics Anonymous is a group of recovering addicts who have found a way to live without the use of drugs. It costs nothing to be a member; the only thing needed is a desire to stop using drugs.
Email: **info@na-ireland.org**

Bereavement and separation

www.barnardos.ie
Barnardos Bereavement Counselling for Children is a service for children and young people run by the Barnardos charity.

Dublin Tel: **01 453 0355**
Email: **bereavement@barnardos.ie**

Cork Tel: **021 431 0591**
Email: **bereavement@cork.barnardos.ie**

Barnardos Bereavement Helpline
Tel: **01 473 2110** (Monday–Friday 10am–12 noon)

The Bereavement Counselling Service
Administration Office, Dublin Street, Baldoyle, Dublin 13
Tel: **01 839 1766**

www.console.ie
Console supports and helps people bereaved through suicide.
Freephone: **1800 201 890**

www.rainbowsireland.com
Rainbows 'spectrum programme' is a service that runs support group programmes for young people who have experienced loss due to bereavement or separation/divorce. The programme is specifically for 12- to 18-year-olds.

The Family Mediation Service is a free mediation service, operated by the Family Support Agency. In the process a trained third party, called a mediator, helps couples to negotiate the terms of their separation with as little conflict as possible.

Tel: **(01) 611 4100**

www.teenbetween.ie

Teen Between is a support service especially for teenagers whose parents are going through a divorce or separation.

Freephone: **1800 303 191**
Email: **teenbetween@mrcs.ie**

Bullying

www.letsomeoneknow.ie

This site has real stories from people who have been bullied and offers advice and support.

www.reachout.com

This offers information and advice on what to do if you are being bullied.

Body image

www.bodywhys.ie

Bodywhys offers support, information and understanding for people with eating disorders.

www.eatingdisorderselfhelp.com

This is a website dedicated to supporting sufferers of eating disorders along the path to recovery.

Exams and careers

www.schooldays.ie

This is a resource for parents and teachers involved in Irish education, including study advice.

www.qualifax.ie

This site gives information on further and higher education and training courses. It also has tips for studying.

Health

www.irishheart.ie

This supports those managing heart disease and strokes.

Locall: **1890 432 787**

www.cancer.ie

This site gives information and support for those who have been diagnosed with cancer or who are affected by someone they know having cancer.

Freephone: **1800 200 700**

Mental health/depression

www.aware.ie

Aware is an organisation that provides information and emotional support to those, and the families of those, who experience depression.

www.console.ie

Console promotes positive mental health within the community in an effort to reduce the high number of attempted suicides and deaths through suicide.

Freephone: **1800 201 890**

www.grow.ie

This helps people who have suffered, or are suffering, from mental health problems.

www.headsup.ie

This is a 24-hour text support and information service provided by Rehab. Text the word 'Headsup' to 50424. A list of topics will be sent to you. Choose a topic and you will instantly be sent a list of confidential Helpline numbers, including where to go for help in a crisis.

www.headstrong.ie

Headstrong works with communities to ensure that young people in Ireland are better supported to achieve mental health and wellbeing. Jigsaw is a community-based service linked to Headstrong.

www.mentalhealthireland.ie

This is a national voluntary organisation that aims to promote mental health and to support people with a mental illness.

www.nosp.ie

The National Office for Suicide Prevention provides information about support services in your area.

www.pieta.ie

Pieta House is a centre that offers help to people thinking about suicide or self-harm.

www.samaritans.org

The Samaritans is a 24-hour, confidential support service for anyone who is experiencing feelings of distress or despair, including those who have thoughts of suicide, and want someone to talk to.
Callsave: **1850 609 090**

www.yourmentalhealth.ie

This provides general information and advice on looking after your mental health.

www.letsomeoneknow.ie

This site gives information to young people on looking after mental health.

www.spunout.ie

Spunout is a web-based movement for young people aged 17–24. It provides them with access to information, support and resources to lead happy, healthy and fulfilled lives.

www.reachout.com

Gives mental health information and includes inspiring real-life stories by young people to help other young people get through tough times.

Pregnancy

www.ifpa.ie

The Irish Family Planning Agency provides information, advice and support to young people about sex, sexual health, relationships and pregnancy.

Puberty

www.childrenfirst.nhs.uk/teens/

This website, run by Great Ormond street Hospital in London, offers a wide range of information to teenagers on topics such as puberty, bereavement and mental health.

www.beinggirl.ie

This site offers girls advice on puberty and relationships (among other things) and an 'Agony Aunt' section where you can ask questions.

Sexuality and sexual health

www.spunout.ie

Spunout is a web-based initiative for young people aged 17–24. It provides young people with access to information, support and resources to lead happy, healthy and fulfilled lives.

www.belongto.org

BeLonG To runs youth groups for Lesbian Gay Bisexual and Transgender (LGBT) young people aged 14 to 18 years. They also have a forum on their website.

Violence

www.childline.ie

Contact Childline for information and support.

Freephone helpline: **1800 666 666**

Text support: Text **list** to **50101**

www.cari.ie

CARI provides a confidential helpline service for anyone with concerns about sexual abuse of a child or young person. CARI also provides a counselling service.

Lo-call helpline: **1890 924567**

Email: **helpline@cari.ie**

www.hse.ie

Contact a social worker at your local HSE health centre. For details of services in your area, call the HSE Infoline.

Lo-call: **1850 24 1850**

www.youth.ie

The National Youth Council of Ireland Child Protection Unit.

www.womensaid.ie

Contact the Women's Aid National Freephone Helpline **1800 341 900** for information on your local domestic abuse support service or refuge.

www.2in2u.ie

This quiz is designed to see if you are in an unhealthy relationship.

www.barnardos.ie

Barnardos offers a variety of specialised services to provide further support to children, parents and families.

Callsave: **1850 222 300**

Email: **info@barnardos.ie**

Key words

Acne
Acne is a disease of the skin where spots occur mainly on the face, but also on the chest and back.

Adolescence
The teenage years when a child starts becoming an adult.

Aggressive
An aggressive communicator communicates his/her views or opinions in an overly forceful manner.

Anti-perspirant
A spray or roll-on cream designed to stop perspiration/sweat.

Assertive
An assertive communicator clearly expresses his/her views in a polite manner.

Binge drinking
The practice of drinking large amounts of alcohol at one time with the aim of getting drunk.

Bullying
Aggressive behaviour by a person or group of people against others. It is usually deliberate and repeated.

Conflict
A disagreement or difference between people.

Drug
A chemical substance that alters the body or mind.

Drug addict
A person who cannot live a normal live without drugs.

Eczema
A skin condition that causes the skin to become red, irritated, itchy, and sometimes develop small, fluid-filled bumps.

Emoticons
Facial expressions shown by punctuation and letters or pictures. They are used to express a writer's mood. They are used in text messages and online messaging.

Heterosexual (straight)
Refers to people who are attracted to others of the opposite sex.

Homosexual (gay/lesbian)
Refers to people who are attracted to others of the same sex.

Menstruation
The monthly shedding of the lining of a woman's uterus, that has built up in preparation for pregnancy.

Misuse
Using something in the wrong way or not for the purpose for which it was intended.

Non-verbal communication
Expressing your feelings through body language or facial expressions such as frowning, slouching and glaring.

Passive
A passive communicator does not express his or her views or opinions.

Puberty
A stage of adolescence when growth and sexual development happens.

Sebum
An oil produced to lubricate the skin.

Self-esteem
How you value yourself.

Sex
Refers to whether you are male or female. Sex is also commonly used as an abbreviation for sexual intercourse.

Sexuality
How you think, act and feel about yourself. Your sexuality depends on your body image, gender, identity, gender roles and sexual orientation. It includes attitudes, values, knowledge and behaviours.

Stereotyping
Putting people into categories or assuming certain groups of people are all alike.

Stretch marks
Fine lines on the body that often occur during puberty due to rapid growth spurts.

Trait
A mannerism or characteristic of a person.

Verbal communication
Saying what it is you want to express.